THE ULTIMATE
air fryer
COOKBOOK

Fry Up Your Favorites, Guilt Free

THE ULTIMATE
air fryer
COOKBOOK

Make way and make room (on your counter) for your new favorite appliance. Everyone loves fried food, but no one wants to eat too much of it as our culture becomes ever more health conscious. Luckily, the air fryer gives you all the crispy, crunchy goodness of a fried comfort-food meal without the frying. That means less fat, less calories, less mess and less sweating in your kitchen over that scalding conventional stove/oven combo. In the following pages, we explain everything you need to know about air frying your way to a tastier, healthier diet—we even provide more than 150 recipes and tips to get you started!

What is an Air Fryer Anyway?

IT'S TIME FOR A BRIEF JOURNEY INTO AIR FRYER 101.

What's It Doing to My Food?

Put very simply, your air fryer is a convection oven specially shaped for countertop cooking. With some cleverly applied hot air, it mimics the crispy feel of fried food without the mess or the added fat. Your food is held in the fryer basket, where the fan moves hot air at high speeds around it. This creates perfectly textured foods like fries, chicken nuggets, onion rings, hot wings and much more. While a traditional oven slowly heats up and then slowly disperses that heat to your food, an air fryer uses rapid air flow to heat up much faster, preventing the soggy fries and burned-on-one-side apps that sometimes come from a traditional oven. The speed at which the heated air moves also helps remove messy mediums like oil. Best of all, because you're not required to add any oil, air frying is just as healthy as baking, but much more delicious.

What Can I Make With It? Also What Can't I Make With It?

Air fryers can be used to cook a wide range of meals and treats. With a few

exceptions, anything you can bake in an oven you can whip up in an air fryer. There are great recipes for everything from chocolate chip cookies to baked cinnamon apples that will highlight your air fryer's versatility. But where the appliance really shines is with making foods we tend to think of as denizens of the deep fryer. Fries, onion rings, mozzarella sticks, egg rolls and spring rolls, fried pickles, chicken legs and wings and all your other favorite fried foods become guilt free in the air fryer without sacrificing taste or texture. As an added bonus, the air fryer works just as well on those frozen Ore-Ida fries as they do on ones you made from scratch, and no one will ever know the difference. What the air fryer can't do is cook from liquid batter unless you freeze that batter first. It's also not the best medium for cooking fresh veggies or cheese. Most air fryers are also pretty small so they can be conveniently stowed, but that means you might have to cook in batches if you're feeding a lot of people at once.

Why Do I Need Another Gadget In My Kitchen?

We know: cabinet space is at a premium in the kitchen and air fryers are about the size of a bread box. It's also an investment of $100+ unless you're lucky enough to find a sale, which is no small amount for something you just heard of. It is, however, an investment of space and cash worth making if, like many Americans, you're trying to cut down on the amount of fried food you eat. The air fryer's ability to perfectly mimic deep fried textures will make it easier for you to eliminate the real deal. If you use a lot of frozen snacks and sides, the air fryer is by far the best medium to use, both quicker and tastier than the same dish in a conventional oven. And best of all, in the summer months the air fryer doesn't heat up your kitchen (or whole place) every time you use it.

The Official Case for Air Fryers

BOBBY DJAVAHERI, PRESIDENT OF YEDI HOUSEWARE APPLIANCES, BRIEFLY EXPLAINS WHY HE'S A TRUE BELIEVER IN THE AIR FRYER AND WHY YOU SHOULD ADD IT TO YOUR ARSENAL.

There are all kinds of ways to prepare your food while cutting down on the amount of extra oil and other fattening fillers that you use. An air fryer, however, is the only one that allows you to keep the same treats on your plate while you eschew the fryer. That's why Bobby Djavaheri thinks everyone should own one.

How did you become aware of air frying?
I first used an air fryer a few years back. I think I ordered it off the television. It

made some amazing chicken tenders and I was hooked. The machine eventually broke down on me, so being part of a family business and taking pride in our brand, Yedi Houseware, we decided to make our own series of air fryers!

What made you think others would feel as you did about the appliance?

Air fryers are beneficial for those in health conscious households, who are using very little oil. Even more, those young professional couples, who work and have children, are coming home and need to whip something up fast. I love the little prep needed to make food. Within minutes of prepping ingredients, you can place your food in the air fryer and dinner is ready in less than 45 minutes! Plus, with all the accessories included, and cheat sheets for how to use the Yedi Air Fryer, the benefits are enormous for any household.

What are your personal favorites to prepare in the fryer?

I love french fries in the air fryer! And of course, chicken tenders, pizza and steak are super delicious!

Maintaining Your Air Fryer

All of the components of your air fryer are dishwasher safe, so remove them and wash separately. Sometimes, food matter can get stuck to the heating elements inside the main body of the heater. These can be removed with a brush.

breakfast

Start your day off with a delicious and guilt-free treat—you'll be glad you did.

Homemade Pop Tarts
Recipe on page 24

Egg Soufflé

15 MINUTES» MAKES 4 SERVINGS
EVERYBODY LIKES TO START THE DAY
WITH A NICE FLUFFY SCRAMBLED EGG, BUT
THIS SOUFFLÉ TAKES THAT FEELING TO
ANOTHER LEVEL.

2 eggs
2 Tbsp heavy cream
1 Tbsp chopped basil
¼ tsp garlic powder
Salt & pepper, to taste

1. Spray 4 ramekins with cooking spray and set aside.
2. Pour the eggs in a bowl with the rest of the ingredients and whisk.
3. Pour the egg mixture into the ramekins.
4. Place the ramekins in the air fryer basket.
5. Set temperature to 380 degrees F and the timer to 10 minutes. Start the air fryer.
6. Once the time is up you're ready to serve.

SHUTTERSTOCK

Ham Egg Rolls

20 MINUTES » MAKES 3 SERVINGS

WHEN YOU'RE PUTTING TOGETHER A REAL BREAKFAST SMORGASBORD, THESE MORSELS WILL BECOME YOUR GUESTS' NEW FAVORITE HAM DELIVERY SYSTEM.

- 6 egg roll wrappers
- 6 slices provolone
- 6 slices deli ham
- 18 slices pepperoni
- 1 cup shredded mozzarella
- Vegetable oil
- ¼ cup freshly grated Parmesan

1. Place an egg roll wrapper on a clean surface in a diamond shape and place a slice of provolone in the center.
2. Top with 1 slice of ham, 3 slices of pepperoni and a large pinch of mozzarella.
3. Fold up bottom half and tightly fold in sides. Gently roll and then seal fold with a couple drops of water.
4. Working in batches, air fry the rolls at 390 degrees F for about 12 minutes until golden. Flip halfway through.
5. Sprinkle with Parmesan, serve and enjoy.

Bacon Egg Muffins

Bacon Egg Muffins

30 MINUTES » MAKES 3 SERVINGS

A GREAT BACON AND EGG BREAKFAST IS CLASSIC FOR A REASON: NOW, YOU CAN TAKE IT ON THE GO MORE EASILY THAN EVER.

6 eggs
¼ tsp brown mustard
¼ cup heavy cream
Salt & pepper, to taste
2 oz shredded cheddar cheese
1 green onion, chopped
2 Tbsp chopped parsley
4 bacon slices, cooked and crumbled

1. Pour the eggs with the mustard, heavy cream, salt and pepper into a bowl and whisk to distribute everything evenly.
2. Evenly divide the cheddar cheese, onions, parsley and bacon into 6 silicone muffin molds.
3. Pour the egg mixture into the muffin molds.
4. Place the silicon molds in the air fryer basket.
5. Set temperature to 330 degress F and the timer to 18 minutes. Start the air fryer.
6. Once the time is up you're ready to serve.

Oatmeal Cakes

30 MINUTES » MAKES 4 CAKES

YOU'VE NEVER HAD ANYTHING LIKE THESE BREAKFAST CAKES BEFORE: AND YOU'LL NEVER GO BACK TO REGULAR HOT CAKES AGAIN.

2 eggs
1 cup milk
1 tsp baking powder
5 tsp brown sugar
2½ cups rolled oats
2 Tbsp olive oil
⅔ cup raisins
½ tsp ground cinnamon
½ tsp salt

1. Spray 4 ramekins with cooking oil and set aside.
2. Add all ingredients into a bowl and mix together until they're properly blended.
3. Evenly pour the oatmeal mixture into the ramekins.
4. Place the ramekins in the air fryer basket.
5. Set temperature at 330 degrees F and the timer to 18 minutes. Start your air fryer.
6. Once the time is up you're ready to serve.

Breakfast

Broccoli Muffins

30 MINUTES » MAKES 6 MUFFINS

EATING YOUR VEGETABLES HAS NEVER
BEEN EASIER THANKS TO THESE DELICIOUS
BROCCOLI MUFFINS.

2 eggs
1 cup milk
1 cup chopped broccoli
2 Tbsp yeast
2 cups flour
1 tsp baking powder
Salt

1. Pour the eggs and the milk into a bowl
and whisk.
2. Add the rest of the ingredients to the
bowl and properly mix.
3. Distribute the mixture into 6 silicone
muffin molds.
4. Place the silicone molds in the air fryer
basket.
5. Set temperature to 330 degrees F and the
timer to 18 minutes. Start the air fryer.
6. Once the time is up you're ready to serve.

Chilaquiles

35 MINUTES » **MAKES 4-6 SERVINGS**
TAKE YOUR MORNINGS SOUTH OF THE
BORDER WITH THIS CLASSIC MEXICAN
BREAKFAST. YOU'LL BE GLAD YOU DID.

½ white onion, grilled
 1 tomato, grilled
 2 green tomatoes, grilled
 2 cups vegetable stock
 ½ can Chipotle peppers
 2 garlic cloves, chopped
 Salt
10 white corn tortillas

For Plating:
1 cup shredded chicken (pre-cooked)
2 Tbsp sour cream
½ pickled red onion
2 poached or fried eggs
1 avocado (optional)
Cilantro (for garnish)

1. After grilling the onion and tomatoes, use
your blender to make the sauce by adding
the onion and tomatoes, vegetable stock,
chipotle, chopped garlic and salt to taste.
Blend it all well, then set aside.
2. Cut each tortilla in 8 equal parts, in
triangles.
3. Air Fry the tortilla triangles, for 8
minutes at 360 degrees F, or until they
reach desired crispiness.
4. For plating, use a bowl and the air fried
tortillas as the base, drizzle with sauce,
and top your Chilaquiles with chicken, sour
cream, pickled red onions, eggs, diced
avocado and cilantro for freshness. Enjoy!

SERGII KOVAL/ALAMY

Homemade Pop Tarts

25 MINUTES » **MAKES 2 SERVINGS**

BELIEVE US: THIS DO-IT-YOURSELF VERSION OF THE CORNER STORE CLASSIC IS WORTH THE TIME AND EFFORT.

1 refrigerated or homemade pie crust
½ cup strawberry jam
Cooking spray
½ cup Greek yogurt, for icing (optional)

1. Lay out pie crust.
2. Using a cookie cutter, cut out two shapes for every pop tart you want to make.
3. Spoon out about 1 Tbsp of jam (more or less depending on the size of your cutout) and spread it within ½-inch of your edge.
4. Carefully place the other cutout on top of your jam and gently press edges together using a fork.
5. Place pop tarts in the air fryer, careful that they are not touching. Spray the top of the pop tarts if you want them to crisp a little more, but it's not necessary.
6. Cook 7 to 10 minutes on 370 degrees F, checking every minute after 6 minutes for desired doneness.
7. They are ready and delicious at that point, but if you want some healthier "icing," mix a dollop of fruit spread and a dollop of Greek yogurt and drizzle over the top!

French Toast

20 MINUTES » MAKES 2 SERVINGS
YOUR BREAKFAST—AND THE CLEANUP—
JUST GOT A WHOLE LOT EASIER.

3 small eggs
4 Tbsp whole milk
1¾ oz caster sugar
2 tsp cinnamon
4 slices brioche

1. Place the egg and milk into a mixing bowl and whisk with a fork.
2. In a shallow bowl mix the sugar and cinnamon and then put to one side.
3. Slice the bread into medium sized pieces and then place into the egg bowl.
4. Make sure each piece of bread is well submerged in the mixture. Then remove any excess liquid from each and place all the bread in the air fryer.
5. Cook for 3 minutes on each side at 360 degrees F.
6. Toss the bread in the sugar and cinnamon and then serve.

JILL CHEN/STOCKSY

Scotch Eggs

30 MINUTES » MAKES 4 SERVINGS

THIS BRITISH FAVORITE HAS GAINED NEW POPULARITY ACROSS THE POND THANKS TO ITS LOW CARB PROFILE AND ON-THE-GO POSSIBILITIES.

1 lb bulk pork sausage
2 tsp coarse-ground mustard, plus more for serving
1 Tbsp finely chopped fresh chives
2 Tbsp finely chopped fresh parsley
1/8 tsp freshly grated nutmeg
1/8 tsp salt
1/8 tsp ground black pepper
4 hard-cooked eggs, peeled
1 cup shredded Parmesan cheese

1. In a large bowl combine sausage, mustard, chives, parsley, nutmeg, salt and black pepper. Gently mix until everything is well combined. Shape mixture into four equal-size patties.
2. Place each egg on a sausage patty and shape sausage around egg. Dip each in shredded Parmesan cheese to cover completely, pressing lightly to adhere. Make sure the cheese shreds are well-pressed into the meat, so they do not fly around in the air fryer.
3. Arrange eggs in air fryer basket. Spray lightly with nonstick vegetable oil. Set fryer to 400 degrees F for 15 minutes. Halfway through cook time, turn eggs and spray with vegetable oil.
4. Serve with coarse-ground mustard.

starters & sides

These small plates are guaranteed to elevate your party, guilt-free.

French Fries
Recipe on page 39

DIY Tortilla Chips

10 MINUTES » MAKES 1 SERVING
AFTER YOU LEARN HOW TO MAKE YOUR OWN, YOU'LL NEVER GO BACK TO THE BIG BAG O' CHIPS AGAIN.

2 6-inch corn tortillas
1 tsp olive oil
Seasoning of choice

1. Preheat air fryer at 350 degrees F.
2. Slice tortillas into quarters.
3. Brush pieces lightly with olive oil and sprinkle with seasoning.
4. Transfer pieces into air fryer basket and fry for 8 minutes or until crisp.

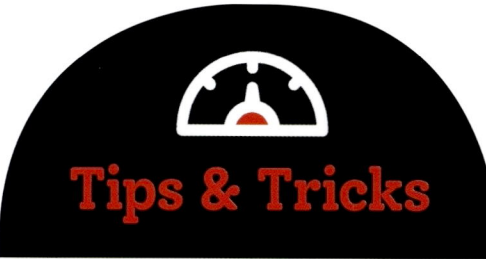

Tips & Tricks

To get your foods to maximum crispiness, you can give them a quick spray of oil about halfway through cooking.

SHUTTERSTOCK

Garlic Parsley
Parm Potatoes

Garlic Parsley Parm Potatoes

20 MINUTES » MAKES 6 SERVINGS

YOU AND YOURS WILL LOVE TUCKING INTO THIS DISH ALMOST AS MUCH AS YOU LOVE TRYING TO SAY ITS NAME FIVE TIMES FAST.

1½ lbs red potatoes
3 Tbsp olive oil
¼ cup grated Parmesan cheese
2 tsp basil
2 tsp Italian seasoning
2 tsp salt
1 tsp pepper
5 tsp minced garlic

1. Cut the red potatoes in half, and then in quarters, so they end up roughly the same size.
2. In a large mixing bowl, mix everything together in with the potatoes, making sure you coat the potatoes.
3. Pour them into the air fryer basket. Set the time for 10 minutes and the temperature at 390 degrees F.
4. When the first 10 minutes are up, flip the potatoes, and set the time for another 8 minutes.
5. Serve with a sprinkle of fresh rosemary. Plate, serve and enjoy!

Mashed Potato Cakes

25 MINUTES » MAKES 5 SERVINGS

WHY SETTLE FOR THE SAME OLD MASH WHEN YOU CAN FRY UP A NEW FAVORITE?

2 cups mashed potatoes
2 cups flour, sifted
1 cup shredded cheddar cheese
2 tsp salt
3 tsp baking powder
1 tsp garlic powder
1 tsp dried basil
4 eggs, beaten
½ cup milk
1 cup breadcrumbs

1. Combine potatoes, sifted flour, cheese, salt, baking powder, garlic powder and basil.
2. Mix together the eggs and milk and stir lightly into the potato mixture.
3. Form into 4- to 5-inch cakes about 1-inch thick.
4. Put breadcrumbs in a flat bottom bowl and press both sides of the potato cakes into the breadcrumbs.
5. Place cakes in the air fryer basket. You should be able to fit 3 or 4 at a time.
6. Mist with a bit of olive oil and close fryer.
7. Bake at 400 degrees F for 10 minutes. Turn after 5 minutes and mist with olive oil and finish for an additional 5 minutes.
8. Serve with sour cream, cheese, chives or your favorite garnish.

AvoKeto Fries

20 MINUTES » MAKES 2 SERVINGS
AVOCADO REPLACES POTATOES FOR A KETO
DIETER'S DREAM, PACKED WITH GOOD FATS.

½ cup (about 2⅛ oz.) all-purpose flour
1½ tsp black pepper
2 large eggs
1 Tbsp water
½ cup panko breadcrumbs
2 avocados, cut into 8 wedges each
Cooking spray
¼ tsp kosher salt
¼ cup no-salt-added ketchup
2 Tbsp canola mayonnaise
1 Tbsp apple cider vinegar
1 Tbsp Sriracha chili sauce

1. Stir together flour and pepper in a shallow
dish. Lightly beat eggs and water in a
second shallow dish. Place panko in a third
shallow dish. Dredge avocado wedges in
flour, shaking off excess. Dip in egg mixture,
allowing any excess to drip off. Dredge in
panko, pressing to adhere.
2. Coat avocado wedges well with cooking spray.
3. Place avocado wedges in the air fryer
basket and cook at 400 degrees F until
golden, 7 to 8 minutes, turning avocado
wedges over halfway through cooking.
Remove from air fryer; sprinkle with salt.
4. While avocado wedges cook, whisk
together ketchup, mayonnaise, vinegar and
Sriracha in a small bowl. To serve, place 4
avocado fries on each plate with 2 Tbsp sauce.

Air-Crispy
French Fries

Air-Crispy French Fries

50 MINUTES » MAKES 3 SERVINGS

PAIR THESE PERFECT SPUDS WITH YOUR FAVORITE SANDWICH (OR JUST GRAB A HANDFUL, NO JUDGMENT).

2 Russet potatoes
1 Tbsp olive oil
1 Tbsp sea salt
½ tsp black pepper

1. Blanch the potatoes in water until tender.
2. Let cool. Cut into fries.
3. Toss with olive oil, salt and pepper.
4. Place the potatoes into the fry basket and then into the air fryer.
5. Scroll to the French Fries setting.
6. Adjust cooking time to 18 minutes at 400 degrees F. You might want to cook in two batches for maximum crispiness.
7. Halfway through cooking, shake the fries.

Tips & Tricks

About 2 Tbsp of water in the bottom of your fry basket will keep the appliance from producing small amounts of smoke while cooking greasy foods.

Corn Zucchini Fritters

35 MINUTES » MAKES 3 SERVINGS

MANY A PLATE HAS BEEN BETTERED BY THE PRESENCE OF THE HUMBLE FRITTER: YOURS IS NEXT.

2 medium zucchinis
1 medium potato, cooked
1 cup corn kernels
2 Tbsp chickpea flour
2-3 garlic cloves, finely minced
Salt & pepper, to taste
1-2 tsp olive oil

For Serving:
Ketchup or yogurt tahini sauce

1. Grate zucchini using a grater or food processor. In a mixing bowl, mix grated zucchini with little salt and leave for 10 to 15 minutes. Then squeeze out excess water from the zucchini using clean hands or using a cheesecloth.
2. Grate or mash the cooked potato.
3. Combine zucchini, potato, corn, chickpea flour, garlic, salt and pepper in a mixing bowl.
4. Roughly take 2 Tbsp batter, shape into a patty and place on parchment paper.
5. Lightly brush oil on the surface of each fritter. Preheat air fryer to 360 degrees F.
6. Place the fritters on the preheated air fryer mesh without touching each other. Cook them for 8 minutes.
7. Turn the fritters and cook for another 3 to 4 minutes or until well done or until you get the desired color.
8. Serve warm with ketchup or yogurt tahini sauce.

Crispy Loaded Potatoes

25 MINUTES » MAKES 4 SERVINGS

THIS IS NOT YOUR MOMMA'S BAKED POTATO, BUT IT IS THE NEW FAMILY STANDARD.

11 oz baby Yukon gold potatoes
    (about eight 2-inch potatoes)
 1 tsp olive oil
 2 center-cut bacon slices
 1½ Tbsp chopped fresh chives
 ½ oz finely shredded reduced-fat
    cheddar cheese (about 2 Tbsp)
 2 Tbsp reduced-fat sour cream
 ⅛ tsp kosher salt

1. Toss potatoes with oil to coat. Place potatoes in the air fryer basket and cook at 350 degrees F until fork tender, 25 minutes, stirring potatoes occasionally.
2. Meanwhile, cook bacon in a medium skillet over medium heat until crispy, about 7 minutes. Remove bacon from pan; crumble.
3. Place potatoes on a serving platter; lightly crush potatoes to split. Drizzle with bacon drippings. Top with chives, cheese, sour cream, salt and crumbled bacon.

Toasty Garlic Bread

20 MINUTES » MAKES 4 SERVINGS

CALLING ALL COMFORT FOOD LOVERS: THIS CHEESY CLASSIC HAS NEVER BEEN EASIER.

1 lb frozen pizza dough
1 Tbsp garlic
1 tsp sea salt
1 Tbsp fresh parsley, chopped
1 Tbsp Parmesan cheese, grated
½ cup olive oil
Marinara sauce

1. Roll the pizza dough out until ½-inch thick.
2. Slice the dough lengthwise, about ¾-inch apart.
3. Roll the dough between your palm and countertop. Make a knot with the dough and repeat until all the dough is used.
4. Add the garlic, spices, cheese and olive oil into a bowl and mix well.
5. Roll the knots into the oil mixture and place into the fry basket. Place into the air fryer.
6. Scroll to the Chicken setting.
7. Set cooking time to 12 minutes at 360 degrees F.
8. Flip over halfway through.
9. Serve with marinara sauce.

Aristocrat's Mac & Cheese

60 MINUTES » MAKES 2 SERVINGS

FEELING A LITTLE TOO GOURMET FOR OUR CLASSIC CHEDDAR CONCOCTION (PG. 158)? THIS WILL KICK YOU RIGHT IN YOUR FANCY PANTS.

2 Tbsp, plus ½ tsp salt
½ pound elbow pasta, or your favorite pasta shape
½ cup whole milk
½ cup heavy cream
½ cup grated Fontina cheese
½ cup grated Gruyere cheese
½ cup grated sharp cheddar cheese
½ tsp Emeril's Original Essence
¼ tsp ground black pepper
⅛ tsp ground nutmeg
¼ cup breadcrumbs
¼ cup finely grated Parmesan cheese
1 Tbsp unsalted butter, melted

1. Fill a large saucepan three-quarters full of water and bring to a boil over high heat.
2. Once boiling, add 2 Tbsp salt to the water and then the pasta.
3. Cook the pasta until just al dente.
4. Remove from the water, drain well and place in a medium bowl.
5. Add the milk, heavy cream, Fontina, Gruyere, cheddar, Essence, remaining ½ tsp salt, black pepper and nutmeg and stir well to combine.
6. Place the pasta into the deep casserole pan, and in a separate small bowl, combine the breadcrumbs, Parmesan cheese and butter and stir to blend. Sprinkle over the top of the pasta and place in the basket of the air fryer and close the drawer.
7. Set temperature to 350 degrees F and the timer for 30 minutes. When the timer goes off, remove the deep casserole pan and allow the mac & cheese to cool for at least 20 minutes before inverting the deep casserole pan over a plate and removing the pan to release the mac & cheese. Cut into wedges and serve warm.

Air-Roasted
Corn

Air-Roasted Corn

20 MINUTES » MAKES 4 SERVINGS

NATURE'S FAVORITE DELIVERY SYSTEM FOR SALT, PEPPER AND BUTTER JUST GOT A MAKEOVER THANKS TO YOUR AIR FRYER.

4 fresh ears of corn
2-3 tsp vegetable oil
Salt & pepper, to taste

1. Remove husks from corn, wash and pat dry. You may need to cut the corn to fit in your basket.
2. Drizzle vegetable oil over the corn, working to cover the corn well with the vegetable oil.
3. Season with salt and pepper. Cook at 400 degrees F for about 10 minutes.

Potato Skins

40 MINUTES » MAKES 5 SERVINGS

OH, WE'RE SORRY, ARE YOU STILL OVEN-BAKING YOUR POTATO SKINS? WELL THEN ALLOW US TO RETORT.

5-10 small baking potatoes, baked ahead of time
½ cup shredded cheddar cheese
½ cup crumbled bacon
Thinly sliced chives
Dean's Bacon Cheddar Dip

1. Season the outside of potatoes with a drizzle of oil and your favorite spices.
2. Bake potatoes ahead of time in your oven.
3. Once the potatoes are done and cool enough to handle, slice each one in half.
4. Scoop out most of the flesh from the inside of the potato. Be sure to leave a good amount around the edges.
5. Sprinkle each half with cheddar cheese and bacon crumbles.
6. Place them in air fryer. Cook for 5 to 7 minutes or until the cheese is melted.
7. Transfer them to a plate and top with chives and bacon cheddar dip.

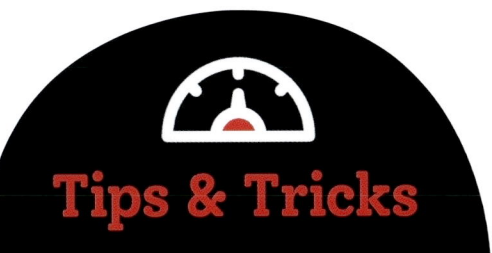

Tips & Tricks

When cooking food items that have to be removed from the fryer at a certain temperature, a quick-read thermometer is an investment that will save you some time and headaches.

Sage & Onion Stuffing Balls

20 MINUTES » MAKES 2 SERVINGS
NEED A QUICK DOSE OF THANKSGIVING? THESE DELICIOUS POPABLES WILL PUT YOU IN THE HOLIDAY SPIRIT ANYTIME.

3½ oz sausage meat
½ small onion, peeled and diced
½ tsp garlic puree
1 tsp sage
3 Tbsp breadcrumbs
Salt & pepper, to taste

1. Place your ingredients into a mixing bowl and mix well.
2. Form into medium sized balls and place them in the air fryer.
3. Cook at 360 degrees F for 15 minutes and then serve. (Serve over pasta if desired.)

Honey Roasted Carrots

15 MINUTES » MAKES 4 SERVINGS
WITH THESE SWEET TREATS, EATING YOUR VEGGIES HAS NEVER BEEN TASTIER.

6 carrots
2 tsp honey
2 tsp chili flakes
1 tsp garlic powder (or crushed garlic)
2 tsp ghee (or coconut oil)
1 Tbsp mint (and/or coriander)
Salt, to taste

1. Peel the skin of the carrots and cut into thin long pieces.
2. Mix honey, chili flakes, garlic, salt and ghee in a bowl.
3. Toss the carrots into it and mix well, making sure the carrots are uniformly coated.
4. Preheat the air fryer at 390 degrees F for 5 minutes.
5. Transfer the prepared carrots to the basket and bake for 5 minutes.
6. Now sprinkle the mint/coriander and mix well.
7. Bake for another minute.
8. Transfer to a serving bowl and serve warm.

Tips & Tricks

Just like with a traditional cooking method, air frying will produce plenty of delicious drippings when you cook with meat, so you can save it for use in later recipes.

Honey Roasted
Carrots

Brussels Sprouts

40 MINUTES » MAKES 3 SERVINGS

NO VEGETABLE HAS GONE FROM ZERO TO HERO AS DRAMATICALLY AS THE SPROUT, AND THIS AIR-FRIED VERSION IS PROOF OF WHY.

1 lb Brussels sprouts
2 tsp avocado oil
1 Tbsp seasoning of choice
Salt & pepper, to taste

1. Preheat the air fryer to 390 degrees F.
2. While the air fryer is heating up, cut the Brussels sprouts in half.
3. Remove the air fryer basket and add the Brussels sprouts, oil and seasonings.
4. Shake it all up to evenly coat everything. Place the basket back in the air fryer.
5. Set the timer for 20 to 30 minutes depending on desired crispiness.
6. Remove the basket from the air fryer every 8 to 10 minutes to shake up the Brussels sprouts so they cook evenly.
7. Once the Brussels sprouts are done cooking, remove them from the air fryer and serve!

Buttery Lemon Green Beans

20 MINUTES » MAKES 4 SERVINGS

WHETHER YOU CALL THEM GREEN BEANS OR STRING BEANS, EVERYONE CAN AGREE ON ONE THING: THE DELICIOUSNESS OF THIS CITRUSY SIDE.

1 lb green beans
2 Tbsp olive oil
Salt & pepper, to taste
2 Tbsp butter
2 cloves garlic, minced
¼ cup lemon juice
1 Tbsp Parmesan cheese

1. Start by washing the green beans, and then cutting the ends off, removing the string from the green beans.
2. Place beans in a large mixing bowl. Lightly coat with olive oil and season with salt and pepper.
3. Put the green beans in air fryer in a single layer at 390 degrees F, for 8 to 10 minutes or until done. Shake halfway through.
4. Meanwhile, make the sauce. In a small saucepan, melt the butter, then mix in the garlic and lemon juice. Heat for about 3 minutes, then mix in the Parmesan cheese and pour over the cooked green beans.

Old-School Okra

35 MINUTES » MAKES 2 SERVINGS

PROVE BEYOND A DOUBT THAT YOUR TABLE HAS SOUL WITH THIS AMAZING VERSION OF A SOUTHERN CLASSIC.

7-8 oz fresh okra
1 egg
1 cup skim milk
1 cup breadcrumbs
½ tsp sea salt
Oil for misting or cooking spray

1. Remove stem ends from okra and cut in ½-inch slices.
2. In a medium bowl, beat together egg and milk. Add okra slices and stir to coat.
3. In a sealable plastic bag or container with a lid, mix together the breadcrumbs and salt.
4. Remove okra from egg mixture, letting excess drip off, and transfer into bag with breadcrumbs. Be sure okra is well-drained before placing it in the breadcrumbs. You may want to use a slotted spoon to lift a little okra at a time and let plenty of the egg wash drip off before putting it into breadcrumbs.
5. Shake okra in crumbs to coat well.
6. Place all of the coated okra into air fryer basket and mist with oil or cooking spray. Okra does not have to be in a single layer, and it isn't necessary to spray all sides at this point. A good spritz on top will do.
7. Cook at 390 degrees F for 5 minutes. Shake basket to redistribute and give it another oil spritz as you shake.
8. Cook for 5 more minutes. Shake and spray again. Cook for 2 to 5 minutes longer or until golden brown and crispy.

Plantains

25 MINUTES » MAKES 2 SERVINGS

TAKE THE AROMAS AND TASTES ON YOUR PLATE TO THE NEXT LEVEL WITH THIS SIMPLE SIDE.

2 ripe plantains (These should be almost all brown and very soft. If it were a banana, you'd say it was no good, but instead, it's a perfect plantain!)
2 tsp neutral oil (We recommend avocado oil, but sunflower or organic canola oil would also be fine.)
⅛ tsp salt (optional, but recommended)

1. Slice your plantains at an angle, cutting pieces that are about ½-inch thick.
2. Toss the plantains, oil and salt together in a medium bowl. Make sure that all of the pieces get coated in oil.
3. Transfer to air fryer basket, and air fry at 400 degrees F for 8 to 10 minutes, shaking after 5 minutes. Your plantains are done when they're browned on the outside and tender on the inside. Cooking time will vary depending on how ripe your plantains are. Check in at 8 minutes, and add another minute or two, if needed, to reach that nice, browned outer layer.

Falafel

30 MINUTES (AFTER SOAKING) » MAKES 3 SERVINGS
AN AUTHENTIC TASTE OF STREET FOOD IN YOUR OWN HOME IS TOUGH TO BEAT: ESPECIALLY WHEN IT'S THIS DELICIOUS.

1½ cups dry garbanzo beans
½ cup chopped fresh parsley
½ cup chopped fresh cilantro
½ cup chopped white onion
7 cloves garlic
2 Tbsp all-purpose flour
½ tsp salt
½ tsp cumin
½ tsp cardamom
½ tsp coriander
½ tsp cayenne pepper

1. For overnight soak: Place dried garbanzo beans in a large bowl and cover with 1 inch of water. Let sit, uncovered, for 20 to 24 hours. Drain thoroughly.
2. For quick soak: Rinse garbanzo beans in a strainer and add to a large pot. Cover with 2 inches of water and bring to a boil. Let boil for 1 minute, cover pot and remove from heat. Let stand for 1 hour. Drain thoroughly.
3. In the bowl of a food processor, add parsley, cilantro, onion and garlic. Mix until well combined.
4. Add soaked garbanzo beans, flour, salt, cumin, cardamom, coriander and cayenne to food processor. Pulse until ingredients form a rough, coarse meal. Scrape down sides of food processor occasionally to ensure all ingredients are combined.
5. Place mixture into a bowl, cover and refrigerate for 1 to 2 hours to allow flavors to come together.
6. Once cooled, remove from refrigerator and form into 1½-inch balls, then flatten balls slightly to form falafel patties.
7. Preheat air fryer to 400 degrees F. Lightly spray fryer basket with oil. Place falafel into basket, being careful not to overcrowd. Cook for 10 minutes, turning halfway through. Repeat with remaining falafel. Serve with your favorite dipping sauce.

SHUTTERSTOCK

Buffalo Cauliflower Nachos

15 MINUTES » MAKES 4 SERVINGS

THE SPICY FLAVOR OF BUFFALO CHICKEN MATCHES PERFECTLY WITH THE NUTRITIOUS BLANK SLATE THAT IS FRESH CAULIFLOWER.

2 cups cauliflower, cut into small florets
2 Tbsp olive oil
½ cup buffalo sauce
¼ cup pinto or black beans
¼ cup corn
3 cups tortilla chips
2 Tbsp chopped red onion
Nacho cheese, for topping

1. Add the cauliflower to a bowl and coat in the olive oil.
2. Add to the basket of the air fryer and cook at 400 degrees F for 10 to 12 minutes, shaking halfway through, until deeply browned and crispy.
3. Remove from the basket into a large bowl and coat in buffalo sauce. On a board or plate add a layer of your chips, then buffalo cauliflower, beans, corn and onion.
4. Pour nacho cheese over the top and add any desired garnishes.

Vegan Cauliflower Tacos

25 MINUTES » MAKES 6-8 TACOS

DON'T LET DIETARY RESTRICTIONS KEEP YOU FROM ENJOYING YOUR FAVORITE SOUTH OF THE BORDER FLAVORS: MAKE THIS EASY AIR FRYER RECIPE INSTEAD.

4 cups cauliflower, cut into bite-sized pieces
1 (19-oz) can of chickpeas, drained and rinsed
2 Tbsp olive oil
2 Tbsp taco seasoning
Avocado slices, cabbage and coconut
    yogurt for tacos

1. Preheat air fryer to 390 degrees F.
2. In a large bowl, toss the cauliflower and chickpeas with the olive oil and taco seasoning.
3. Dump the florets and chickpeas into the basket of air fryer.
4. Cook in the air fryer, shaking the basket occasionally, for 20 minutes, or until cooked through. Cauliflower should be golden but not burnt.
5. Serve in taco shells with avocado slices, cabbage and coconut yogurt (or regular yogurt).

Vegan Cauliflower Tacos

Crab Cakes

Crab Cakes

2 HOURS, 30 MINUTES » MAKES 4-6 CAKES
AN AUTHENTIC TASTE OF THE EAST
COAST IS NEVER FAR AWAY FROM YOUR
TABLE THANKS TO THESE CLASSICS.

¾ lb crab meat

2 eggs

2 cups panko (you may replace with
   breadcrumbs)

1 tsp Worcestershire sauce

1 tsp Dijon mustard

1 onion, chopped

2 tsp mayonnaise

Salt & pepper, to taste

½ cup parsley

1. Combine all ingredients in a bowl and mix
until they're fully blended.
2. Cover and let sit in fridge for 2 hours.
3. Make 4 to 6 patties from the crabmeat mix.
4. Place the patties on the air fryer basket.
5. Set the temperature to 350 degrees F and
the timer to 15 minutes.
6. Start air fryer. Serve with your favorite
sauce, or place on a bun for crab cake
sandwiches.

Crispy Zucchini

25 MINUTES » MAKES 4 SERVINGS
GET THE SATISFYING CRUNCH OF A
FRIED POTATO, AND A JUICY SERVING OF
VEGGIES THANKS TO ZUCCHINI.

2 zucchini

1 Tbsp chopped fresh parsley

2 Tbsp breadcrumbs

4 Tbsp grated Parmesan cheese

1 Tbsp vegetable oil

Pepper, to taste

1. Slice the zucchini in half lengthwise and cut
each piece in half again through the middle.
You'll end up with 8 pieces of zucchini.
2. Place the zucchini into the air fryer basket
and lightly spray with vegetable oil.
3. Cook at 350 degrees F for 5 minutes.
4. Mix together the parsley, breadcrumbs,
cheese, oil and freshly ground black pepper to
taste.
5. Once the 5 minutes are done, take out the
basket and top the zucchini with the mixture.
6. Slide the basket into the air fryer and
set the timer for 10 more minutes. Fry the
zucchini gratin until the timer rings or the
gratin is golden brown, then serve.

Cauliflower Tots

15 MINUTES » MAKES 6-8 SERVINGS

GIVING CARBS A REST? THERE'S NO REASON TO GIVE UP YOUR FAVORITE SIDE DISHES, LIKE THESE TASTY TOTS.

Cooking spray
4 cups cauliflower florets, steamed
   (about ½ large cauliflower)
1 large egg, lightly beaten
1 cup shredded cheddar
1 cup freshly grated Parmesan
⅔ cup panko breadcrumbs
2 Tbsp freshly chopped chives
Salt & pepper, to taste

1. Rice the cauliflower in a food processor. Place the riced cauliflower on a kitchen towel and squeeze to drain water.
2. In a mixing bowl, pour the cauliflower and mix with all the other ingredients.
3. Spoon about 1 Tbsp of the mixture and roll it into a tater-tot shape with your hands.
4. Place the tater tots in the air fryer basket.
5. Cook at 375 degrees F for 10 minutes, until tots are golden.
6. Serve with ketchup. Enjoy.

Roasted Garlic

~~~~~~~~~~

20 MINUTES » MAKES 6 SERVINGS

WHEN YOUR DINNER ABSOLUTELY NEEDS A FLAVORFUL DOSE OF UMAMI, GO FOR THIS CAN'T MISS ROASTED GARLIC.

1 large head of garlic
Aluminum foil
Drizzle of olive oil (1-2 Tbsp)
Salt & pepper, to taste

1. Place the head of garlic on a piece of aluminum foil, drizzle with a little olive oil, and season with salt and pepper. Wrap the head of garlic in the foil.
2. Place in the basket of air fryer and cook on 400 degrees F for 10 minutes. Check the garlic after 10 minutes. The cloves should be soft and caramelized when done. If the garlic is not soft, it might not brown with the covered foil, so carefully open the top of the foil and continue to cook at 5-minute intervals. If after the first 5 minutes the garlic has not cooked much, increase time to 7-minute intervals.
3. Cool the garlic for 10 minutes and remove the cloves by squeezing them out of the paper skins. Or you can use a butter knife to scoop them out, place them in a small dish until ready to use. The garlic should spread like a paste, and it is delicious on toasted bread, as a topper for vegetables or even as a complement to a grilled steak.

JEFFTAKESPICS2/ALAMY

Onion Flower

15 MINUTES » MAKES 1 ONION FLOWER
YOU DON'T HAVE TO GO OUT TO EAT FOR
THIS FAMOUS STARTER: NOW YOU CAN
MAKE IT IN YOUR OWN HOME.

1 yellow onion
1 Tbsp sea salt
1 Tbsp pepper
1 cup almond flour
1 oz coconut flakes
¾ cup sun-dried tomato oil

For Plating:
¼ cup each of:
Guacamole
Ricotta cheese
Sun-dried tomato oil
Dijon mustard

1. Slice a whole onion in a star formation.
Using a large bowl, add the onion and open it
up like flower. Sprinkle the sea salt, pepper,
almond flour, coconut flakes and oil and rub it
all over the onion flower making sure to get it
all in every crevice.
2. Using an oven safe bowl, place inside
air fryer and cook at 360 degrees F for 12
minutes.
3. After 12 minutes, carefully remove your
onion flower from the air fryer. Serve with
sides of guacamole, ricotta cheese, sun-
dried tomato oil, dijon mustard or any of your
favorite sauces.

Stuffed Garlic Mushrooms

15 MINUTES » MAKES 3 SERVINGS
ADD THIS SAVORY TREAT TO YOUR
APPETIZER SPREAD THE NEXT TIME YOU
ENTERTAIN AND YOUR GUESTS WILL
THANK YOU FOR IT.

1 Tbsp breadcrumbs
1 Tbsp olive oil
1 tsp garlic puree
1 small onion, peeled and diced
1 tsp parsley
Salt & pepper, to taste
6 small mushrooms

1. Add the breadcrumbs, olive oil, garlic,
onion, parsley and salt and pepper to a bowl,
then mix.
2. Clean your mushrooms and remove the
middle stalks. Fill the middle area with your
breadcrumb mixture.
3. Add the mushrooms to the air fryer basket,
then cook at 350 degrees F for 10 minutes.

SHUTTERSTOCK

snacks & small bites

Amuse your bouche with these air-fried plates to tide you over until the big meal.

Banana Chips
Recipe on page 80

Air-Fried Pickles

35 MINUTES » MAKES 4 SERVINGS
PARDON OUR PUN, BUT THIS NEW TAKE ON A GAMEDAY FAVORITE IS DEFINITELY A VERY BIG DILL.

32 dill pickle slices
½ cup all-purpose flour
½ tsp salt
3 large eggs, lightly beaten
2 Tbsp dill pickle juice
½ tsp cayenne pepper
½ tsp garlic powder
2 cups panko breadcrumbs
2 Tbsp snipped fresh dill
Cooking spray

1. Preheat the air fryer to 400 degrees F. Let pickles stand on a paper towel until liquid is almost absorbed, about 15 minutes.
2. Meanwhile, in a shallow bowl, combine flour and salt. In another shallow bowl, whisk eggs, pickle juice, cayenne and garlic powder. Combine panko and dill in a third shallow bowl.
3. Dip pickles in flour mixture to coat both sides; shake off excess. Dip in egg mixture, then in crumb mixture, patting to help coating adhere.
4. Spritz pickles and the air fryer basket with cooking spray.
5. Working in batches if needed, place pickles in a single layer in the air fryer basket and cook until golden brown and crispy, about 10 minutes.
6. Turn pickles; spritz with additional cooking spray. Continue cooking until golden brown and crispy, about 10 minutes.
7. Serve immediately. If desired, serve with ranch dressing.

Zucchini Chips

50 MINUTES » MAKES 3 SERVINGS
THE POTATO HAS TAKEN US FAR IN THE CHIP GAME—IT'S ZUCCHINI'S TURN AT BAT.

2 medium zucchinis,
   sliced according to your preference
¾ tsp garlic salt
1 large egg
½ cup Parmesan cheese, grated
½ cup breadcrumbs
1 tsp Italian seasoning
Pepper, to taste
Cooking spray

1. Prepare the zucchini for cooking by slicing into strips or thin discs. Toss in salt and let sit for 30 minutes to remove the excess moisture. Rinse with cold water and then pat dry with paper towels.
2. Preheat air fryer to 390 degrees F.
3. Whisk the egg in a bowl and mix the cheese, breadcrumbs and Italian seasoning in another. These will serve as your breading.
4. Cover each zucchini slice with the breading by first dipping into the egg bath and then in the breadcrumbs mix.
5. Spray some cooking oil into the fry basket then place the zucchini slices inside. You can also opt to drizzle olive oil onto the slices to achieve a fried taste.
6. Cook for about 10 minutes or until crispy.
7. Sprinkle with pepper and serve with your dip of choice.

Crispy Fried Frankfurters

12 MINUTES » MAKES 2 SERVINGS

THE RECIPE COULDN'T BE SIMPLER: NEITHER COULD THE SHEER JOY OF THIS CHILDHOOD CLASSIC.

2 hot dogs
2 hot dog buns
2 Tbsp grated cheese if desired

1. Preheat air fryer to 390 degrees F for about 4 minutes.
2. Place two hot dogs into the air fryer, cook for about 5 minutes.
3. Remove the hot dog from air fryer.
4. Place the hot dog on a bun, add cheese if desired.
5. Place dressed hot dog into the air fryer and cook for an additional 2 minutes.

Tips & Tricks

Aerosol sprays have been known to interact poorly with the coating used in air fryer baskets, so opt for another lubrication method before you get cooking.

Your New Favorite Blueberry Muffins

15 MINUTES » MAKES 5 SERVINGS

YOU MIGHT HAVE THOUGHT THE BLUEBERRY MUFFIN WAS SIMPLY TOO GOOD TO BE IMPROVED UPON. WE ALL MAKE MISTAKES.

2½ cups self-rising flour
½ cup monk fruit (or your preferred sugar)
½ cup cream
¼ cup avocado oil (or any light cooking oil)
1 lemon, juiced
2 eggs
1 tsp vanilla
1 cup blueberries
Brown sugar for topping (a little sprinkling on top of each muffin—less than a teaspoon)

1. In small bowl, mix the self-rising flour and sugar together. Set aside.
2. In a medium bowl, combine cream, oil, lemon juice, eggs, vanilla and blueberries.
3. Add the flour mixture to the liquid mixture and stir just until blended.
4. Spoon the batter into silicone cupcake holders. Sprinkle ½ tsp brown sugar on top of each muffin.
5. Bake at 320 degrees F for 10 minutes, checking muffins at 6 minutes to ensure they are not cooking too fast. Put a toothpick into the center of the muffin and when the toothpick comes out clean and the muffins have browned, they are done. No need to over-bake the muffins, they will continue to cook for another minute or two after they are removed from the air fryer.
6. Remove and let cool before serving.

Your New Favorite
Blueberry Muffins

Old Bay Chicken Wings

50 MINUTES » MAKES 6 SERVINGS
GET AN AUTHENTIC TASTE OF THE ATLANTIC COAST WITH THESE FLAVORFUL ALTERNATIVES TO BUFFALO WINGS.

3 lbs chicken wing parts
¾ cup potato starch
1 Tbsp Old Bay seasoning
½ cup butter
1 tsp True Lemon seasoning
Fresh lemon slices

1. Pat dry chicken wing parts.
2. Mix together potato starch and Old Bay seasoning. Add chicken wings and coat.
3. Shake off excess potato starch and place in air fryer basket.
4. Cook at 360 degrees F for 35 minutes, shaking often. Turn temperature to 400 degrees F and cook an additional 10 minutes, shaking often.
5. Melt butter with True Lemon and toss with hot wings. Serve wings with the remaining lemon butter for dipping and lemon slices for squeezing.

SHUTTERSTOCK

Dry Rub Hot Wings

65 MINUTES » MAKES 2 SERVINGS

BRING THE HEAT WITHOUT THE NEED
FOR A BOX OF WET NAPS WITH THESE
CAYENNE-FUELED CLASSICS.

1 lb chicken wings, fresh or frozen, thawed
2 Tbsp paprika
2 Tbsp white sugar
1 Tbsp basil
1 Tbsp oregano
1 Tbsp garlic powder
1 Tbsp onion powder
1 Tbsp thyme
1 Tbsp white pepper
1 Tbsp black pepper
1 Tbsp cayenne pepper

1. Preheat air fryer to 400 degrees F for 4 to
5 minutes.
2. Add spices and sugar together in a bowl.
3. Stir well.
4. Dip each wing into the mix and rub both
sides of the wings.
5. Place the wings in a bowl and allow to
marinate for 30 to 45 minutes.
6. Arrange chicken wings in a single layer in
the air fryer.
7. Air fry at 400 degrees F for 12 minutes.
8. At the halfway point, flip the wings for
even cooking.

Apple Chips

20 MINUTES » MAKES 2 SERVINGS

THESE TASTY CHIPS CAN BE USED AS
PART OF AN APPETIZER OR CHARCUTERIE
PLATTER, OR THEY CAN BE EATEN BY THE
BOWLFUL. TRUST US.

1 apple, peeled, cored and thinly sliced horizontally
½ tsp ground cinnamon
1 Tbsp sugar
Pinch of kosher salt

1. Preheat your air fryer to 390 degrees F.
2. Lay the apple slices on a baking sheet. In
a small bowl, stir together the cinnamon,
sugar and salt. Sprinkle the mixture evenly
over the apple slices.
3. Working in batches, place the apple slices
in the fry basket and insert into the air fryer.
Cook until the slices are slightly golden
brown, 7 to 8 minutes, turning them over
halfway through cooking.
4. Transfer the chips to a bowl and let cool
before serving.

Tips & Tricks

The more you overcrowd the
basket, the less surface area of
your food will be exposed to the
rapidly moving air, so make sure
to work in small batches.

Apple Chips

Crispy Chickpeas

Crispy Chickpeas

25 MINUTES » MAKES 3 SERVINGS

TOSS A FEW OF THESE OVER A SALAD OR TRY A FEW WITH YOUR FAVORITE SANDWICH INSTEAD OF CHIPS.

1 can chickpeas
  (drained and rinsed—no sugar added)
2 tsp olive oil
1 tsp ground cumin
1 tsp ground coriander
1 tsp garlic powder
$\frac{1}{8}$ tsp ground ginger

1. Put the rinsed beans into a medium mixing bowl and add the rest of the ingredients.
2. Stir well to coat the beans in the oil and spices.
3. Pour the beans into the food basket of the air fryer.
4. Adjust the air fryer to a temperature of 370 degrees F.
5. Cook for 12 minutes.
6. Pull out the basket and stir the beans. Put the basket back in and set again at 370 degrees F and cook for another 8 minutes.
7. Repeat the stirring process one more time, set for 370 degrees F and cook for 1 minute longer.
8. If your beans are large they may need a little longer to get a good crunch. At this point, cook and stir in 1 minute intervals until they are cooked to your liking. The main idea is to stir them every few minutes throughout the process. They should have a nice little crunch to them when they have cooled.
9. Pack them in snack bags and take them with you or store them in the fridge for up to one week. But be aware that you may have to roast them again for a minute or two to get them crunchy again if they've been in the fridge awhile. Enjoy!

Mini Spanakopita Bites

20 MINUTES » MAKES 3 SERVINGS

WHIP UP A BATCH OF THESE GREEK FLAVOR BOMBS ON A SUNDAY FOR ALL-WEEK SNACKING, OR PULL OUT ALL THE STOPS FOR THE NEXT BIG GAME.

1 (10-oz) bag frozen chopped spinach
1 (4-oz) package feta cheese
2 eggs, beaten
Salt and pepper to taste
2 (1.9-oz) mini phyllo shells

1. Thaw your frozen spinach. Then drain as much liquid out of the spinach as you can.
2. Mix the drained spinach with feta, eggs, salt and pepper.
3. Spoon the combined mixture into the phyllo shells. (To prevent them from flying around, put the filled pies into a muffin tin.)
4. Set the temperature to 220 degrees F and the time for 4 minutes. Check to make sure they are hot and bubbling. If not, add another 3 minutes.
5. Remove from the air fryer, plate, serve and enjoy!

Beet Chips

30 MINUTES » MAKES 3 SERVINGS
BEAT THE BOREDOM OF PLAIN OLD CRISPS
WITH THE POWER OF THE BEET.

4 small beets, about ½ lb total, peeled
2 tsp extra-virgin olive oil
Kosher salt and freshly ground pepper, to taste

1. Slice the beets very thinly, about $\frac{1}{16}$-inch
thick. Line a baking sheet with paper towels
and arrange the beet slices on the towels in a
single layer. Top with another layer of paper
towels and press down firmly. Set aside for 10
minutes to allow the beets to dry.
2. In a large bowl, toss the beet slices with
the olive oil and a generous pinch each of
salt and pepper.
3. Preheat air fryer to 300 degrees F. Spray
the air fryer basket with nonstick cooking
spray, then arrange half of the beets in the
basket in a single layer. Insert into the air
fryer and cook until the beets are crisp and
browned at the edges, 12 to 15 minutes.
Transfer the beet chips to a platter and
repeat to air fry the remaining beets. Serve
immediately.

Prawn Crackers

10 MINUTES » MAKES 5 SERVINGS
ADD DEPTH TO THIS FAVORITE FROM ACROSS THE POND BY WORKING WITH YOUR AIR FRYER.

3 cups dried prawn crackers
1 Tbsp oil

1. Preheat the air fryer to 390 degrees F.
2. In a large mixing bowl, add oil to dried prawn crackers.
3. Toss and ensure that all pieces are coated thoroughly with the oil.
4. Divide the crackers and air fry in batches (about 3 pieces per batch).
5. Air fry for about 2 to 3 minutes at 390 degrees F or until golden brown. Pull out the basket and shake halfway during frying (or use a tong to "stir").
6. Continue with the remaining batches until all the crackers are fried.
7. Cool and store in airtight container.

Banana Chips

30 MINUTES » MAKES 4 SERVINGS
BE HONEST: THESE LITTLE BEAUTIES ARE JUST ABOUT THE ONLY REASON YOU BUY TRAIL MIX. CUT OUT THE MIDDLEMAN WITH YOUR AIR FRYER.

3-4 ripe bananas
½ tsp turmeric powder
1 tsp salt, plus more for seasoning
1 tsp of your preferred cooking oil
½ tsp chaat masala
Honey, as desired

1. Peel the bananas and keep aside.
2. Prepare a mixture of water, turmeric powder and salt. Cut slices of banana into this mixture. It will prevent the bananas from turning black and also give a nice yellow color.
3. Keep bananas soaked in this mixture for 5 to 10 minutes.
4. Drain the water and dry the slices.
5. Apply a little oil on slices to prevent them sticking together in the air fryer.
6. Preheat the air fryer at 350 degrees F for 5 minutes.
7. Air fry the chips for about 15 minutes at 350 degrees F.
8. Add salt, chaat masala and honey.

Tips & Tricks

When air frying bite sized items like banana chips or french fries, be sure to shake the basket occasionally during cooking to make sure all sides of the pieces are exposed to the hot air directly.

THE GOLD(EN BROWN) STANDARD

FOR THE FINEST AIR-FRIED MEALS, JUST FOLLOW THESE TIPS.

Preheat Your Fryer

Just like a regular oven, or an Olympic athlete, the air fryer benefits from a few minutes to warm up. For the perfect preheat settings for your favorite dishes, you can always check out the helpful hints on *yedihousewareappliances.com*.

Keep It Lubricated

Conversely, just like a regular frying pan, your air fryer will need oil in a light coating to prevent stickage. Nonstick cooking sprays, however, can damage the fry basket, so according to the fine folks at Yedi, it's best to avoid them.

Add Water to Fatty Foods

To prevent your food from smoking too much in the fry basket, just put a little water in along with bacon and other fatty treats. As a bonus, Yedi recommends using the resulting drippings in your saucemaking adventures.

Shake It Up, Baby

To make sure all sides of your food are getting perfectly golden brown, give the fry basket a shake or two at regular intervals while cooking.

Practice Food Distancing

Don't overcrowd that fry basket: To make that fryer work at its best, there needs to be plenty of air flow throughout cooking, so give everything room to breathe.

For more tips and techniques as well as can't miss air fryer recipes, including how-to videos, check out *yedihousewareappliances.com*.

Air-Fry Eggplant Fritters

70 MINUTES » MAKES 3 SERVINGS
PAIR THESE PERFECT MORSELS WITH
TOMATO SAUCE OR YOUR FAVORITE DIP FOR
A SATISFYING NOSH.

1 medium (1–1¼ lbs.) eggplant,
   sliced into strips
¾ tsp garlic salt
2 large eggs
½ cup wheat germ, toasted
½ cup Parmesan cheese, grated
1 tsp Italian seasoning
2 Tbsp olive oil or cooking spray

1. Slice the eggplant up according to your
desired fry size and length, then add some
garlic salt for seasoning. Let sit for up to 45
minutes to remove excess moisture.

2. Preheat air fryer to 400 degrees F.

3. In one bowl, whisk the eggs. In another,
mix the wheat germ, cheese and seasonings.
These will serve as your breading.

4. Dip the sliced eggplants into the egg and
then cover it with the breading.

5. Spray the cooking basket with some
cooking oil. Place the eggplant slices inside
the fry basket and cook for 5 to 7 minutes
before turning over the ingredients. Make
sure not to overcrowd your fry basket when
cooking this dish as it needs better air
penetration due to the breading.

6. Turn and cook for another 5 to 7 minutes
or until the eggplant fritters are crispy.

BBQ Chicken Wings

4 HOURS, 15 MINUTES » MAKES 3 SERVINGS

A PROTEIN PACKED SNACK THAT WON'T SPOIL YOUR APPETITE FOR THE BIG MEAL, A COUPLE OF THESE BBQ CLASSICS WILL KILL YOUR HUNGER PANGS.

12 chicken wings, separated
2 Tbsp ground ginger
2 tsp sesame oil
⅔ cup apple cider vinegar
4 tsp minced garlic
½ cup brown sugar
1 cup soy sauce

1. Mix all ingredients except chicken wings in a bowl until combined.
2. Add chicken wings to the mixture and marinate up to 4 hours.
3. Lightly grease the air fryer basket before placing chicken in at 400 degrees F for 15 minutes.
4. Flip the wings halfway through cooking.
5. Serve with BBQ sauce.

SHUTTERSTOCK

Healthy Popcorn

15 MINUTES » MAKES ONE LARGE BOWL
YOU'LL NEVER GO BACK TO THE BAGGED
VERSION AGAIN AFTER YOU AIR FRY YOUR
OWN KERNELS.

3 Tbsp corn kernels
Avocado oil
Salt & pepper, to taste
Chives and nutritional yeast (for garnish)

1. Spread kernels in the fryer basket and
spray lightly with avocado oil.
2. Air fry at 390 degrees F for about 15
minutes, checking every few minutes for
burning kernels and turning off the fryer
when popping sound stops.
3. Put the finished popcorn in a bowl and
garnish with chives and nutritional yeast
after another light spray of oil.

Pita Pizza

10 MINUTES » MAKES 1 SERVING
THE PERFECT AFTER-SCHOOL SNACK IS
ALSO THE PERFECT BITE FOR A PECKISH
GROWN-UP.

1 pita bread
1 Tbsp marinara sauce
¼ cup mozzarella cheese
1 drizzle extra virgin olive oil

1. Use a spoon and swirl marinara sauce onto
pita bread.
2. Add cheese on top.
3. Add a little drizzle of extra virgin olive oil
over top of pizza.
4. Place in air fryer pizza pan and then place
in air fryer basket.
5. Cook at 350 degrees F for 6 minutes.
6. Carefully remove from air fryer and cut.

LARRY PETERSON/E+/GETTY IMAGES

Buffalo Drumsticks

20 MINUTES » MAKES 3 SERVINGS

CAN'T GET ENOUGH SPICE IN YOUR LIFE? TRY THESE CHICKEN WINGS THAT PACK PLENTY OF PUNCH THANKS TO A GENEROUS HELPING OF HOT SAUCE.

1 lb chicken drumsticks
½ cup hot sauce

1. Brush drumsticks with hot sauce.
2. Lightly grease the air fryer basket before placing chicken in at 400 degrees F for 15 minutes.
3. Flip the drumsticks halfway through cooking.

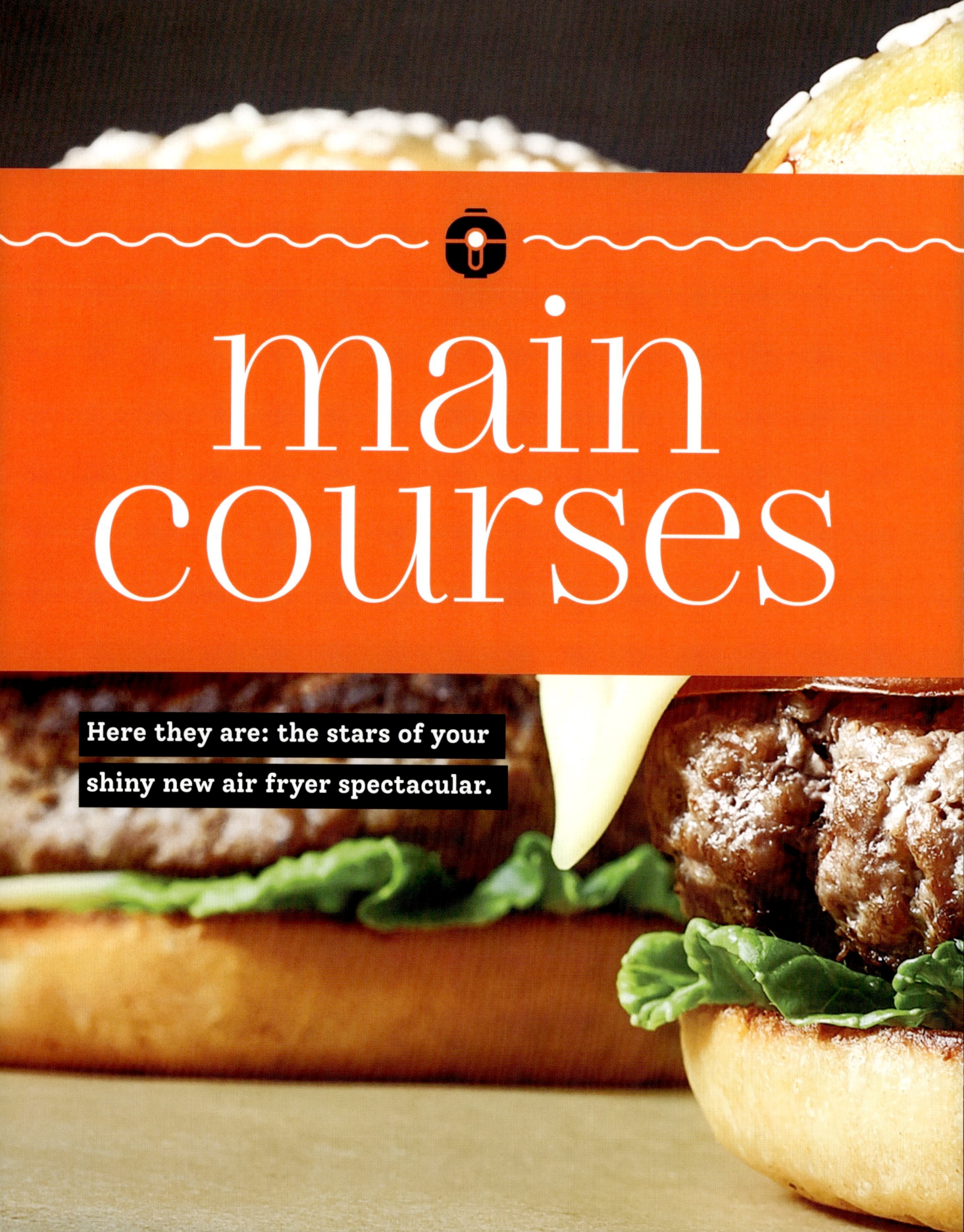

main courses

Here they are: the stars of your shiny new air fryer spectacular.

All-American Burgers
Recipe on page 97

Country-Style Air-Fried Steak

30 MINUTES » MAKES 4 SERVINGS
YOU AND YOURS WILL LOVE ALL THE
DOWN-HOME COMFORT WITH ALMOST
NONE OF THE GUILT.

2 lbs rib eye steak
1 Tbsp steak rub
1 Tbsp olive oil

1. To preheat the air fryer, scroll to the
French Fries setting.
2. Adjust the cooking time to 4 minutes at
400 degrees F to preheat.
3. Season the steak on both sides with rub
and olive oil.
4. Place the steak in the fry basket.
5. Scroll to the Steak setting.
6. Adjust cooking time to 14 minutes at 400
degrees F.
7. After 7 minutes, flip the steak.
8. When the timer is done, remove steak
from the air fryer. Let rest for 10 minutes
before slicing and serving.

SHUTTERSTOCK

All-American Burgers

20 MINUTES » MAKES 4 SERVINGS

WHEN IT'S TOO COLD OUTSIDE TO FIRE UP THE GRILL, LOOK NO FURTHER THAN THESE AIR-FRIED CLASSICS.

1 Tbsp Worcestershire sauce
1 tsp Maggi seasoning sauce
Liquid smoke (few drops)
½ tsp garlic powder
½ tsp onion powder
½ tsp salt (or salt sub)
½ tsp ground black pepper
1 tsp parsley (dried)
1 lb ground beef

1. Set air fryer temperature to 350 degrees F.
2. In a small bowl, mix together all the seasoning items, from the Worcestershire sauce down to and including the dried parsley.
3. Add this to the beef in a large bowl.
4. Mix well but be careful not to overwork the meat as that leads to tough burgers.
5. Divide the beef mixture into 4 and shape the patties. With your thumb, put an indent in the center of each one to prevent the patties from bunching up in the middle.
6. Put patties in the air fryer and spray tops of patties lightly with oil.
7. Cook 10 minutes for medium (or longer to desired degree of doneness). There is no need to turn the patties.
8. Serve hot on a bun with toppings of your choice.

The Holiday Turkey of the Future

75 MINUTES » MAKES 16 SERVINGS

REMEMBER THAT TIME YOUR CRAZY UNCLE ALMOST BURNED THE HOUSE DOWN WITH HIS D.I.Y. DEEP FRYER? NEVER AGAIN.

8 lbs turkey breast, bone-in
2 Tbsp sea salt
1 Tbsp black pepper
2 Tbsp olive oil

1. Season the turkey and rub with olive oil.
2. Place the turkey breast side down in the fry basket.
3. Scroll to the Chicken setting.
4. Adjust cooking time to 20 minutes at 360 degrees F.
5. When the timer is done, carefully turn the breast over.
6. Scroll to the Chicken setting.
7. Adjust cooking time to 20 minutes at 360 degrees F.
8. Test the turkey with a thermometer for proper doneness (165 degrees F).
9. Let turkey rest 20 minutes before serving.

Not Your Nonna's Italian Meatballs

40 MINUTES » MAKES 5 SERVINGS

THEY'D NEVER HEARD OF AN AIR FRYER WHEN SHE LEARNED TO MAKE THEM, BUT THAT DOESN'T MEAN YOU HAVE TO CHOOSE AN INFERIOR METHOD.

2 lbs ground beef (choose your preferred cuts)
2 large eggs
1¼ cups breadcrumbs
   (or 3 slices of slightly stale bread made into
   crumbs with grater or food processor)
¼ cup chopped fresh parsley
1 tsp dried oregano (optional)
¼ cup grated Parmigiano-Reggiano
1 small clove garlic, chopped
Salt & pepper, to taste
1 tsp light oil dabbed on a paper towel
   to coat the air fryer basket
Rosemary, to garnish

1. Place the meat and all the ingredients in a large mixing bowl.
2. Mix all the ingredients together with your hands. You can use a wooden spoon to begin the mixing process but using your hands is the best way to blend everything together. Mix the ingredients just until everything is well blended.
3. Scoop up a small handful of meat and roll in the palm of your hand to your desired size meatball (approximately 2-inch round). Or you can use a cookie scoop which will give you even-sized meatballs.
4. Lightly coat the air fryer basket with light oil, spread on with a paper towel.
5. Cook meatballs at 350 degrees F for 10 to 13 minutes until lightly browned. Turn them over and cook another 4 to 5 minutes. Remove to a plate when baked.
6. When ready, place meatballs into a tomato sauce to continue cooking until sauce is done.
7. Garnish with rosemary and serve on a hero roll or with your favorite pasta.

Cheesy Chicken
Quesadillas

Cheesy Chicken Quesadillas

15-20 MINUTES » MAKES 2 SERVINGS
TURN TACO TUESDAY ON ITS HEAD WITH THESE AIR-FRIED 'DILLAS.

4 soft taco shells
⅓ cup shredded Mexican cheese
1 package frozen chicken fajita strips
½ cup sliced green peppers
½ cup sliced onions
Salsa (optional)
Sour cream (optional)

1. Preheat air fryer on 370 degrees F for about 3 minutes.
2. Spray cooking basket lightly with vegetable oil.
3. Place 1 soft taco shell in the basket.
4. Place shredded cheese on shell. You can use as much or as little as you'd like.
5. Lay out fajita chicken strips so they are in a single layer. Put your onions and green peppers on top of your chicken. Add more shredded cheese.
6. Place another soft taco shell on top and spray lightly with vegetable oil. You can use the rack that came with the air fryer on top of the shell to hold it in place.
7. Set timer for 4 minutes.
8. Flip over carefully with a large spatula.
9. Spray lightly with vegetable oil and place rack on top of shell to hold it in place.
10. Set timer for 4 minutes. If it's not crispy enough for you, leave in for a couple of extra minutes.
11. Remove and cut into 4 slices or 6 slices.
12. Serve with salsa and sour cream if desired.

Tofu Delight

30 MINUTES » MAKES 3 SERVINGS
TAKE YOUR HEALTH FOOD TREND TO THE FAR EAST AND TEACH YOUR FAMILY THE DELIGHTS OF SOYBEANS.

1 block tofu, chopped into 1-inch pieces
2 Tbsp soy sauce
2 Tbsp olive oil, divided
1 tsp turmeric
½ tsp garlic powder
½ tsp onion powder
½ cup chopped onion
2½ cups chopped red potato, 1-inch cubes, (about 2-3 potatoes)
4 cups broccoli florets

1. In a medium-sized bowl, toss together the tofu, soy sauce, 1 Tbsp olive oil, turmeric, garlic powder, onion powder and onion. Set aside to marinate.
2. In a separate, small bowl, toss the potatoes in the remaining olive oil, and air fry at 400 degrees F for 15 minutes, shaking once around 7 to 8 minutes into cooking.
3. Shake the potatoes again, then add the tofu, reserving any leftover marinade. Set the tofu and potatoes to cook at 370 degrees F for 15 more minutes and start the air fryer.
4. While the tofu is cooking, toss the broccoli in the reserved marinade. If there isn't enough to get it all over the broccoli, add a little bit of extra soy sauce. Dry broccoli is not your friend. When there are 5 minutes of cooking time remaining, add the broccoli to the air fryer.
5. Serve in hot tomato sauce if desired.

BBQ Ribs

20-30 MINUTES » MAKES 6 SERVINGS
ENJOY ALL THE FLAVOR WITH LESS MESS
AND MORE TIME WITH THE FAMILY.

2-3 lbs baby back ribs
32 oz BBQ sauce (your favorite)
Salt & pepper, to taste

1. Start by preheating your air fryer to 390
degrees F. (You don't have to preheat, but it
might give the ribs more flavor.)
2. Season the ribs with salt and pepper
and other spices if you like. Remove the
membrane.
3. Smother your ribs with BBQ sauce and
place them in your air fryer basket.
4. Set the timer for 10 minutes, flip, then
cook for another 7 minutes.
5. Remove from the air fryer, add some extra
sauce if you wish, plate, serve and enjoy!

NOTE *You should always use a thermometer
for pork, as eating raw pork can cause illness.*

Tips & Tricks

Just like regular ovens, air
fryers can run a little hot or
cold depending on the model
and the conditions you're
cooking in. So get to know your
machine as best you can.

Chicken Tikka

Main Courses

Chicken Tikka

20-30 MINUTES » MAKES 3 SERVINGS

THERE'S A REASON THIS DISH IS THE BEST-SELLER AT YOUR LOCAL INDIAN RESTAURANT. NOW YOU CAN RECREATE IT AT HOME.

1 lb chicken thighs, cut into bite-size cubes
½ cup Greek yogurt
1 tsp curry powder
1 tsp garam masala
½ tsp smoked paprika
¼ tsp cayenne pepper (optional)
1 Tbsp olive oil
1 tsp salt
Oil spray or mist
1 large green pepper,
  cut into large chunks (optional)
1 large red onion, chopped (optional)
Lemons and cilantro to garnish

1. In a large bowl or a resealable bag, combine the cubed chicken, yogurt, curry powder, garam masala, smoked paprika, cayenne pepper (if using), olive oil and salt. Give it a good mix and marinate, in the fridge, anywhere between 2 hours to overnight.
2. If using wooden skewers, soak them in water for 2 hours.
3. Skewer each chicken piece, alternating with green pepper chunks and red onion chunks, onto metal or soaked wooden skewers.
4. Lightly grease the air fryer basket.
5. Add the skewers to the basket and air fry at 360 degrees F for 15 minutes.
6. Serve the Chicken Tikka with a squeeze of lemon juice and a sprinkling of chopped cilantro.
NOTE It pairs great with Indian basmati rice or any kind of Indian bread like naan or even pita bread.

Reuben Calzones

30 MINUTES » MAKES 2 SERVINGS

CAN'T DECIDE ON WHICH NEW YORK STAPLE YOU'RE CRAVING? EMBRACE THE MELTING POT AND COMBINE THE TWO.

1 (13.8-oz) tube refrigerated pizza crust
4 slices Swiss cheese
1 cup sauerkraut, rinsed and well drained
½ lb sliced cooked corned beef
Thousand Island salad dressing

1. Preheat air fryer to 400 degrees F. Spritz air fryer basket with cooking spray.
2. On a lightly floured surface, unroll pizza crust dough and pat into a 12-inch square. Cut into four squares. Layer one slice of the cheese and a fourth of the sauerkraut and corned beef diagonally over half of each square to within ½-inch of edges. Fold one corner over filling to the opposite corner, forming a triangle; press edges with a fork to seal. Place two calzones in a single layer in greased air fryer basket.
3. Cook until calzones are golden brown, 8 to 12 minutes, flipping halfway through cooking. Remove and keep warm; repeat with remaining calzones. Serve with salad dressing.

Marinated Steak

15 MINUTES » MAKES 2 SERVINGS
KICK THE FLAVOR UP ON YOUR EVERYDAY CUTS WITH THIS FLAVORFUL RECIPE.

2 New York strip steaks, any cut
1 Tbsp low-sodium soy sauce
1 tsp liquid smoke
1 Tbsp McCormick's Grill Mates Montreal Steak seasoning or steak rub (or season to taste)
½ Tbsp unsweetened cocoa powder
Salt & pepper, to taste
Melted butter (optional)

1. Drizzle the steaks with the soy sauce and liquid smoke. You can do this inside zip top bags.
2. Season the steak with the seasonings.
3. Refrigerate for at least a couple of hours, preferably overnight.
4. Place the steak in the air fryer. Do not use any oil. Cook two steaks at a time (if air fryer is standard size). You can use an accessory grill pan, a layer rack or the standard air fryer basket.
5. Cook for 5 minutes at 375 degrees F. After 5 minutes, open the air fryer and examine your steak. Cook time will vary depending on your desired doneness. Check the inside of the steaks to determine if they have finished cooking. You can stick a knife or fork in the center to review the level of pink. You can also use a meat thermometer and cook to 125 degrees F for rare, 135 degrees F for medium-rare, 145 degrees F for medium, 155 degrees F for medium-well and 160 degrees F for well done.
6. For medium steak, at 5 minutes, flip the steak and cook for an additional 2 minutes, for a total of 7 minutes cook time using the air fryer.
7. Remove the steak from the air fryer and drizzle with melted butter.

Crispy Pollock

20 MINUTES » MAKES 2 SERVINGS
SERVE THIS ALONGSIDE CHIPS FOR A FANCY
THROWBACK TO THE BRITISH ISLES.

2 pollock filets
Salt & pepper, to taste
1 egg, whisked
½ cup breadcrumbs, plus more if needed

1. Season the fish with salt and pepper.
2. Let sit for 10 minutes.
3. Dredge through the egg and then cover
with the breadcrumbs and place in spray-
oiled air fryer.
4. Cook at 370 degrees F for 8 minutes.

SHUTTERSTOCK

Tips & Tricks

To ensure that your air
fryer operates at its best,
allow at least five inches on all
sides for air flow. And never,
ever put anything on top of
your air fryer.

Cauliflower Pizza

30 MINUTES » MAKES 2 SERVINGS

WE ALL LOVE PIZZA, BUT MORE AND MORE OF US DON'T LIKE CARBS. PROBLEM SOLVED WITH THIS CAULI CRUST CLASSIC.

½ **package organic riced cauliflower, steamed**
2 **whole eggs**
1 **cup mozzarella**
1 **Tbsp Flavor God Garlic Lovers seasoning,**
  or whatever seasoning you like
¼ **cup psyllium powder**
Pizza toppings, whatever you prefer

1. Steam your riced cauliflower in the microwave until it is tender, about 3 to 4 minutes.
2. Put cauliflower in a strainer and push out as much water as you can using the back of a spoon.
3. Preheat air fryer for 5 minutes at 400 degrees F.
4. Put all of the ingredients into a bowl except the psyllium. Mix together.
5. Start adding the psyllium as you are mixing. When the mix starts to look dry you are done.
6. Put "dough" into air fryer being careful not to burn yourself. Flatten it out to your desired thickness and so it's not quite touching the edges.
7. Cook in air fryer at 400 degrees F for 10 to 15 minutes until it is golden brown.
8. Put your preferred toppings on the pizza crust and put back in the air fryer to melt the cheese.

Zoodles and Meatballs

30 MINUTES » MAKES 3 SERVINGS

WHO NEEDS CARBS? NOT YOU, NOW THAT YOU HAVE THIS ZOODLE-BASED RECIPE.

1 lb ground beef
3 Tbsp flaxseed meal (optional)
1 dash liquid smoke (optional)
1 dash McCormick Montreal Steak Seasoning (or whatever you prefer)
1 cup spaghetti sauce
2 medium zucchini, spiralized

1. Mix ground beef, flaxseed meal, liquid smoke and seasoning. Form into meatballs and place in the air fryer basket.
2. Set the air fryer to meat presetting and let your fryer do its magic! You'll want to check on your meatballs a little over the halfway point to roll them around a bit for even cooking.
3. Put the spaghetti sauce in a small saucepan and warm or reduce as you like it, over low heat.
4. Zoodle up your zucchini. If you don't have a tabletop or handheld spiralizer, you can use a julienne peeler or even a mandoline.
5. With about 5 minutes left on your meatballs and after you've rolled them about the fryer basket, pile your zoodles on top.
6. Cook a couple of minutes, and then pop open the air fryer and flip the zoodles. When the zoodles are warm, "al dente" texture and maybe have a hint of browning, consider them done.
7. Serve it up. Heats up great for leftovers (if you have any left, that is).

Pub Standard Mince Pies

25 MINUTES » MAKES 2 SERVINGS

IT DOESN'T GET MORE OLD SCHOOL THAN THIS BIT OF ENGLISH PUB FOOD. GIVE YOUR GUESTS A HISTORY LESSON WITH THEIR DELICIOUS DISH.

½ lb plain flour
¼ lb butter
1 oz caster sugar
¼ lb mincemeat
1 medium egg, beaten

1. Preheat the air fryer to 350 degrees F
2. Start by making your sweet pastry. In a mixing bowl, mix your butter into your flour until it resembles fine breadcrumbs. Add the sugar and mix well. Add a little warm water at a time while mixing at the same time until your mixture makes lovely soft dough.
3. Roll out your pastry using a little extra flour to stop it sticking. Place pastry into each of the pastry cases that you're using. Then fill each one with mincemeat.
4. Add another layer of pastry on top and then slit with a knife so the mince pies have room to breathe. Brush the top with egg.
5. Place in the air fryer for 12 minutes at 350 degrees F.

Tuna Cutlets

15 MINUTES » MAKES 2 SERVINGS

SURE, YOU COULD GO FOR A TUNA-MAYO SALAD ON WHITE BREAD. BUT WHY WOULD YOU WHEN YOU'RE JUST A FEW MINUTES AWAY FROM THIS AMAZING DISH?

½ Tbsp oil, plus more for brushing
1 onion, chopped
1 green chile, seeded and chopped
1 Tbsp grated ginger
1 can albacore tuna, strained
1 medium sized potato, boiled
2 Tbsp celery
1 cup breadcrumbs
1 egg
Salt, to taste

1. Heat ½ Tbsp oil in a frying pan and saute chopped onions, green chile and ginger for a few minutes. As soon as the onions turn translucent, add the drained tuna to the pan and fry till all the liquid gets absorbed.
2. Remove the tuna to a plate and let it cool down. Add mashed potato and chopped celery, adjust salt and mix well to make the cutlet patty dough.
3. Make balls of the dough and shape them.
4. Beat the egg in a bowl and spread the breadcrumbs on a plate. Roll each cutlet in breadcrumbs, dip in egg and roll in crumbs again.
5. Arrange the cutlets in a preheated air fryer tray, brush lightly with oil and run the air fryer for about 2 to 3 minutes. Apply oil again with a brush on the cutlets and allow them to get crispy golden. This will take about 4 to 5 more minutes.
6. Serve the cutlets hot on top of crackers if desired.

Main Courses

Herb Salmon

20 MINUTES » MAKES 2 SERVING

IF YOU'VE NEVER HAD AIR-FRIED FISH BEFORE, THIS CRISPY SALMON IS THE PERFECT INTRODUCTION.

1 tsp lime zest
1 Tbsp olive oil
1 Tbsp minced rosemary
1 Tbsp minced thyme
1 Tbsp minced garlic
1 salmon fillet

1. Mix lime zest, olive oil, rosemary, thyme and garlic in a bowl.
2. Rub salmon with the herb mixture.
3. Place the salmon on the air fryer basket.
4. Air fry at 400 degrees F for 18 minutes.
5. Serve over your favorite rice, pasta or potato dish.

SHUTTERSTOCK

Thai Thighs

20 MINUTES » MAKES 4 SERVINGS

PEANUT BUTTER IS THE SECRET
INGREDIENT IN THESE TASTY THIGHS: BUT
YOU DON'T HAVE TO TELL YOUR GUESTS.

⅓ cup peanut butter
½ cup hot water
1 tsp minced ginger
1 Tbsp lime juice
1 minced garlic clove
2 Tbsp sweet chili sauce
1 Tbsp soy sauce
1 Tbsp hot sauce
½ tsp salt
1 lb chicken thighs
Sesame seeds, for garnish

1. Add all ingredients except chicken thighs
to a bowl and mix.
2. Add the chicken thighs into the bowl. Seal
and allow it to marinate overnight.
3. Lightly grease the air fryer basket.
4. Place the chicken thighs on the air fryer
basket and air fry at 400 degrees F for 15
minutes
5. Halfway through, take out the basket and
flip the chicken thighs using a pair of tongs.
6. Put the air fryer lid basket back on and
resume cooking.
7. Serve with sesame garnish.

Seasoned Tilapia

20 MINUTES » MAKES 2 SERVINGS

FISH LIKE TILAPIA ARE A PERFECT DELIVERY SYSTEM FOR ALL YOUR FAVORITE SPICES.

1 tilapia fillet
½ sliced lemon
¼ tsp dried thyme
¼ tsp dried oregano
½ tsp garlic powder
½ tsp fresh lemon juice
1 tsp olive oil
Salt & pepper, to taste

1. In a small bowl, mix together all ingredients besides fillet.
2. Rub the mixture on the fillet and let it sit in the fridge for 1 hour.
3. Place the fillet in the air fryer basket.
4. Air fry at 400 degrees F for 18 minutes.
5. Serve over salad or rice.

SERGII KOVAL/ALAMY

Main Courses

Sweet and Sour Pork

〜〜〜〜〜〜〜〜〜

20 MINUTES » MAKES 3 SERVINGS

YOU DON'T NEED TO ORDER OUT TO ENJOY YOUR FAVORITE CHINESE-AMERICAN DISHES NOW THAT YOU'VE GOT AN AIR FRYER.

¾ lb pork eye
Salt & pepper, to taste
½ cup crushed pineapple
½ cup cider vinegar
½ cup brown sugar
¼ cup ketchup
1 Tbsp soy sauce
1½ tsp Dijon mustard
½ tsp garlic powder

1. Sprinkle pork with salt and pepper.
2. Place pork on greased tray in air-fryer basket.
3. Set the air fryer temperature to 350 degrees F and start cooking the pork until it begins to brown around edges, 7 to 8 minutes.
4. Combine all the other ingredients in a bowl and mix.
5. Pour into a pan over medium heat and bring to a boil. Lower heat and simmer, uncovered, until thickened, about 6 to 8 minutes, stirring occasionally
6. Serve pork with sauce.

Turkey Patties

〜〜〜〜〜〜〜〜〜

2 HOURS, 30 MINUTES » MAKES 4 SERVINGS

FOR A LEANER PROTEIN ON YOUR BURGER, THESE TURKEY PATTIES ARE PERFECT.

1 lb ground turkey
½ cup breadcrumbs
½ tsp minced garlic
2 Tbsp lemon juice
1 egg
2 Tbsp chopped cilantro
Salt & pepper, to taste

1. Add all ingredients in a bowl and mix until they're fully blended.
2. Cover and let it sit in fridge for 2 hours.
3. Make 4 patties from the turkey mix.
4. Air fry at 360 degrees F for 25 minutes.
5. Halfway through, flip the patties using a pair of tongs.
6. Serve on a bun with all your favorite fixings.

Coconut Shrimp

15 MINUTES » MAKES 3 SERVINGS

FANCIFY YOUR SHRIMP WITH THE HELP OF TROPICAL FLAVORS COURTESY OF MANGO AND COCONUT.

12 jumbo shrimp
 5 oz garlic goat cheese
 3 oz flour
 1 egg, beaten
3½ oz coconut flakes
3½ oz panko breadcrumbs
   Sea salt

Mango Sauce:
 1 mango
½ lemon, juiced
 5 oz Chardonnay
½ cup basil, mint & cilantro, mixed

For Plating:
Sautéed oyster mushrooms
Sautéed king oyster mushrooms

1. Peel the shrimp and clean the upper part of them.
2. Cut in butterfly and stuff them with the garlic goat cheese (if you can't find flavored goat cheese, you can mix the cheese with roasted garlic, herbs, salt & pepper to add flavor).
3. Create a prep space with three bowls. One for the all-purpose flour, one for a beaten egg and one with the coconut flakes and panko mixed together. Dip each of the shrimp in the flour, egg and panko mix.
4. Once all shrimp have been breaded, sprinkle with sea salt. Air fry the shrimp for 12 minutes at 350 degrees F or until desired crispiness to taste.
5. For the mango sauce, using a house blender, blend the mango, lemon juice, wine, basil, mint, cilantro and top with sea salt to bring all the flavors forward.
6. For plating, serve the coconut shrimp over a bed of oyster and king oyster mushrooms, drip with mango sauce to your heart's content, and top with fresh basil for decoration.

SHUTTERSTOCK

Main Courses

Smoky Pork Chops

25 MINUTES » MAKES 2 SERVINGS

NOTHING SAYS DOWN-HOME COOKING LIKE A SMOKY PIECE OF PORK. THESE AIR FRIED VERSIONS ARE SOMETHING SPECIAL.

1 large egg
¼ cup milk
1 Tbsp yogurt
1 cup panko or breadcrumbs
1 Tbsp salt
1 Tbsp pepper
1 cup finely grated pecans
2 smoked boneless pork chops
¼ cup all-purpose flour

1. In a shallow bowl whisk together eggs, milk and yogurt. In another shallow bowl toss together panko (or breadcrumbs), salt, pepper and grated pecans.
2. Coat pork chops with flour; shake off excess. Dip in egg mixture; shake off excess, then place in crumb mixture, patting to help adhere.
3. Working in batches as needed, place chops in a single layer in air fryer basket.
4. Cook at 360 degrees F for 20 minutes, turning halfway through cooking. Remove and keep warm. Repeat with remaining chops.

Eggplant Parmesan

15 MINUTES » MAKES 3 SERVINGS

ONE OF YOUR FAVORITE CHECKERED-TABLECLOTH ITALIAN CLASSICS IS AT ITS BEST WHEN IT COMES RIGHT OUT OF YOUR AIR FRYER.

1 large eggplant, sliced
½ cup panko breadcrumbs
2 Tbsp Parmesan cheese
Salt & pepper, to taste
Garlic powder, to taste
Onion powder, to taste
½ cup flour
½ cup milk
1 cup marinara sauce
½ cup shredded mozzarella

For Serving
4 oz spaghetti or pasta of your choosing,
   cooked al dente (about 2 oz per person)
1¼ cups breadcrumbs
   (or 3 slices of slightly stale bread made into
   crumbs with grater or food processor)
Parsley for garnish

1. Wash, dry and remove stems of eggplant. Cut into slices.
2. Mix the panko with Parmesan, salt, pepper, garlic and onion powders.
3. Dip the eggplant slices into flour, then milk and finally, the panko mixture.
4. Spray lightly with oil (if desired) and place into the basket of air fryer at 390 degrees F for 15 minutes, flipping halfway through, spraying the second side lightly.
5. While the eggplant is cooking, go ahead and cook your pasta.
6. Once golden on both sides, spoon on some of the marinara and top with a combination of the two cheeses. Cook just until the cheese begins to melt.
7. Serve with the pasta and extra sauce. Garnish with breadcrumbs and parsley.

SHUTTERSTOCK

Garlic Turkey Breasts

45 MINUTES » MAKES 4-6 SERVINGS

FOR A FLAVORFUL SPIN ON A CLASSIC DINNER, JUST ADD GARLIC!

2 lbs turkey breast
Salt & pepper, to taste
4 Tbsp melted butter
3 cloves garlic, minced
1 tsp chopped thyme
1 tsp chopped rosemary

1. Season the turkey breasts on both sides with salt and pepper.
2. In a small bowl, combine melted butter, garlic, thyme and rosemary.
3. Brush the turkey breasts with the butter mix.
4. With the skin side up, air fry at 375 degrees F for 40 minutes or until internal temperature reaches 160 degrees F.
5. Remember to flip the turkey halfway through the cooking.
6. Take out of the air fryer and let sit for 5 minutes before slicing.
7. Serve over mashed potatoes or rice.

Main Courses

Steak Kebabs

45 MINUTES » MAKES 4 SERVINGS
RAIN MESS WITH YOUR COOKOUT PLANS?
AIR FRY THESE DELECTABLE KEBABS.

1 lb sirloin steak cut into 1-inch chunks
¼ cup olive oil
¼ cup soy sauce
1 Tbsp minced garlic
1 tsp brown sugar
½ tsp ground cumin
¼ tsp salt
¼ tsp black pepper
8 oz baby bella mushrooms, stems removed
1 green bell pepper, chopped into 1-inch pieces
1 red onion, chopped into 1-inch pieces

1. Combine steak, olive oil, soy sauce, garlic, brown sugar, cumin, salt and black pepper. Allow to marinate for 30 minutes.
2. Place marinated meat, baby bella mushrooms, green pepper and red onion on skewers.
3. Preheat air fryer to 390 degrees F. Once preheated, place skewers inside of air fryer. Cook for 10 to 12 minutes, flipping halfway.
4. Serve alongside your favorite kebab sauces and pita.

FOOD DRINK AND DIET/MARK SYKES/ALAMY

Main Courses

Chili Fajitas

15 MINUTES » MAKES 4 SERVINGS

ARE YOUR TASTE BUDS IN THE MOOD FOR A TRIP SOUTH OF THE BORDER? GIVE THEM WHAT THEY WANT WITH THESE FAJITAS.

1 lb sliced beef
1 tsp garlic powder
1 tsp paprika
1½ tsp cumin
½ Tbsp chili powder
3 Tbsp olive oil
½ sliced onion
2 sliced bell peppers
Salt & pepper, to taste

1. Add all ingredients together in a bowl and mix thoroughly.
2. Lightly grease the air fryer basket.
3. Place the mixture in the air fryer basket. Air fry at 400 degrees F for 8 minutes.
4. Serve with hot sauce if you like things spicy.

Crumbled Chicken

20 MINUTES » MAKES 2 SERVINGS

THIS TENDER DELICIOUS CHICKEN DISH
TASTES BEST OUT OF THE AIR FRYER.

2 boneless chicken breasts
Salt & pepper, to taste
1 tsp paprika
1 Tbsp olive oil
1½ cups crumbled crackers

1. Season the chicken breasts with salt,
pepper and paprika before coating with olive
oil and crumbled crackers.
2. Lightly grease the air fryer basket.
3. Place the chicken breasts on the air fryer
basket. Air fry at 400 degrees F for 15
minutes.
4. Halfway through, take out the basket and
flip the chicken using a pair of tongs.
5. Put the air fryer lid basket back on and
resume cooking.
6. Serve with your favorite sauces on the side.

Honey Mustard Salmon

15 MINUTES » MAKES 2 SERVINGS

THE SWEET FLAVORS OF THIS DISH WILL TURN EVEN THE MOST ARDENT SEAFOOD HATERS ON THEIR HEADS.

1 Tbsp Dijon mustard
1 Tbsp honey
1 tsp soy sauce
Salt & pepper, to taste
1 salmon fillet

1. In a small bowl, mix mustard, honey, soy sauce and salt and pepper.
2. Pour mixture over salmon and work into the flesh.
3. Place the salmon in the air fryer basket.
4. Air fry at 400 degrees F for 14 minutes.
5. Serve over your favorite rice, pasta or potato dish.

Shrimp Parm

20 MINUTES » MAKES 3 SERVINGS

YOU'LL HAVE A HARD TIME GOING BACK TO REGULAR OLD CHICKEN CUTLETS AFTER YOU EAT THIS SEAFOOD VERSION.

4 cloves garlic, minced
$2/3$ cup Parmesan cheese, grated
1 tsp pepper
½ tsp oregano
1 tsp basil
1 tsp onion powder
2 Tbsp olive oil
2 lbs jumbo cooked shrimp, peeled and deveined
Lemon, quartered

1. In a large bowl, combine garlic, Parmesan cheese, pepper, oregano, basil, onion powder and olive oil.

2. Gently toss shrimp in mixture until evenly coated.

3. Spray air fryer basket with non-stick spray and place shrimp in basket.

4. Cook at 350 degrees F for 8 to 10 minutes or until seasoning on shrimp is browned.

5. Squeeze the lemon over the shrimp before serving.

SHUTTERSTOCK

Beef Empanadas

20-30 MINUTES » MAKES 8 SERVINGS
SWITCH UP YOUR RED MEAT DELIVERY
METHOD BY OPTING FOR THESE
WONDERFUL POCKETS OF FLAVOR.

8 Goya® empanada discs (in frozen section),
   thawed
1 cup picadillo
1 egg white, whisked
1 tsp water

1. Preheat the air fryer to 325 degrees F for
8 minutes. Spray the basket generously with
cooking spray.
2. Place 2 Tbsp picadillo in the center of
each empanada disc. Fold in half and use
a fork to seal the edges. Repeat with the
remaining dough.
3. Whisk the egg whites with water, then
brush the tops of the empanadas.
4. Bake 2 or 3 at a time in the air fryer for 8
minutes, or until golden. Remove from heat
and repeat with the remaining empanadas.

Main Courses

Cornish Game Hen

50 MINUTES » MAKES 4 SERVINGS

A CLASSIC GAME BIRD WITH SOME CLASSIC SEASONING—A RECIPE FOR SUCCESS.

1–2½ lbs Cornish hen
1 cup buttermilk
1 cup seasoned flour
2 eggs, lightly beaten
1 cup panko breadcrumbs
Coconut oil spray

1. Rinse and place Cornish hen in a zip top bag with enough buttermilk to cover. Place bag in a bowl to prevent leakage. Refrigerate for 2 to 24 hours.
2. Set up a dipping station with seasoned flour, egg and panko.
3. Remove hen from buttermilk, allowing the excess buttermilk to drip off. Discard buttermilk. Dredge hen in the seasoned flour making sure to cover the entire hen. Then dip hen into the beaten eggs, and finally coat with the panko.
4. Spray lightly with coconut oil spray for extra crispy skin.
5. Place hen in air fryer and cook for 30 minutes at 360 degrees F or until internal temperature is 165 degrees F.
6. Allow to rest for about 5 minutes and serve with your favorite side dish.

SHUTTERSTOCK

Salmon Patties

15 MINUTES » MAKES 2 SERVINGS
FRESH SALMON ISN'T JUST DELICIOUS, IT'S GREAT FOR YOU. SO DIG IN AND FEEL GOOD ABOUT IT.

14¾ oz canned salmon
1 egg
¼ cup diced onion
1 tsp dill weed
½ cup breadcrumbs

1. Start by cleaning the fish, remove the bones and skin.
2. Mix the egg, onion, dill weed and breadcrumbs into the salmon.
3. Mix well.
4. Shape into patties. Place them in the air fryer.
5. Set the temperature for 370 degrees F. Cook for 5 minutes, flip and air fry for another 5 minutes.
6. Plate, serve and enjoy!

Tips & Tricks

The air fryer is at its best when making tasty meals for one or two people. While it can handle more in batches, making air fryer food for the whole clan can be time consuming, so plan accordingly.

comfort classics

One of the many benefits of the air fryer is that you can indulge in favorites with less guilt. So dig into these old standards and leave room for dessert!

Classic Mac & Cheese
Recipe on page 158

Pizzeria-Style Hot Wings

35 MINUTES » MAKES 3 SERVINGS

WHETHER IT'S GAME DAY, COOKOUT NIGHT OR JUST TO SATISFY A CRAVING, THESE HOT WINGS HAVE THE FLAVOR SEALED IN WITH AIR FRYING.

12 raw chicken wings (drumettes and
   flats, according to your preference)
 1 cup buffalo sauce

1. Place the wings into the fry basket.
2. Scroll to the French Fries setting.
3. Adjust cooking time to 25 minutes at 400 degrees F.
4. Halfway through cooking, flip the wings.
5. When done, remove and toss with buffalo sauce.
6. Return the wings to the air fryer. Scroll to the French Fries setting and cook for 8 more minutes at 400 degrees F.

Tips & Tricks

When it comes to reheating, ditch your microwave. Leftovers from the air fryer taste much better (and are much less soggy).

SHUTTERSTOCK

Fried Oysters

45 MINUTES » MAKES 2 SERVINGS

FOR A PO' BOY TOPPING OR A PERFECT FINGER FOOD FOR YOUR NEXT COOKOUT, AIR FRY SOME SHUCKED GOODNESS.

 2 large eggs
 3 Tbsp hot sauce
½ cup all-purpose flour
½ tsp Creole or Cajun seasoning
 1 cup panko or breadcrumbs
12 plump fresh oysters, shucked
Salt & pepper, to taste
Cooking oil spray

1. In one bowl, whisk the eggs and hot sauce together. Put the flour and seasoning in another. Crush the panko or breadcrumbs a bit finer and then place them in a third shallow bowl.
2. Grab a baking sheet and line it with parchment paper.
3. Cover the oysters first in flour, then shake off the excess before dipping each piece in the egg mixture. Again, shake the excess before rolling them around in the breadcrumbs.
4. Place all of the oysters on the baking sheet. Once they're all lined up, refrigerate for 30 minutes.
5. Spray oil lightly on the fry basket before placing the refrigerated oysters inside.
6. Set the air fryer to 400 degrees F for 2 minutes then start cooking. Shake the fry basket occasionally, checking the doneness of the oysters as you do.
7. Once done, remove from the fry basket and sprinkle with salt.
8. Serve on a po' boy or over greens.

County Fair Corn Dog Nuggets

25 MINUTES » MAKES 2 SERVINGS

YOU DON'T HAVE TO WAIT FOR YOUR FAVORITE STAND NEXT TO THE TILT-A-WHIRL TO OPEN UP—MAKE YOUR FAVORITE CARNIVAL SNACK AT HOME WITH LESS GREASY GUILT!

 2 hot dogs, uncured
 2 large eggs
1½ cups crushed cornflakes
½ cup all-purpose flour
Cooking spray
12 bamboo skewers or craft sticks
 8 tsp yellow mustard

1. Slice each hot dog into halves then cut them up into three portions. Insert a bamboo skewer or wooden stick into each piece.
2. Crack the eggs and whisk in a shallow bowl, then place the crushed cornflakes in another. Put the flour in a third separate shallow bowl.
3. Dip each hot dog into the flour first then the egg and last into the cornflakes bowl. Try to press the cornflakes into the hot dog a bit so the small bits will stick.
4. Lightly spritz some cooking oil into the fry basket then place the corn dogs inside.
5. Set the air fryer to 375 degrees F and cook for 5 minutes. Turn the corn dogs and then resume cooking for 5 more minutes or until the breading becomes crispy.
6. Serve with mustard.

Western Frittata

15 MINUTES » MAKES 1 SERVING
YOU'LL FEEL LIKE YOU'RE AT YOUR
FAVORITE GREASY SPOON—WITHOUT THE
GREASE—WHEN YOU DIG INTO THIS HEARTY
BREAKFAST.

1 Tbsp melted butter
1 breakfast sausage patty
2 large eggs
Salt & pepper, to taste
1 Tbsp chopped spring onions
1 Tbsp chopped bell peppers
2 Tbsp cheddar cheese

1. Generously grease a 4-inch cake pan or a
mini loaf pan (or any oven safe pan that fits
in your air-fryer basket) with butter.
2. Chop up the breakfast sausage and place
in the greased pan. Air fry at 350 degrees F
for 5 minutes.
3. Meanwhile, in a medium sized bowl, crack
the eggs. Add salt and pepper and whisk well.
4. Add the chopped spring onion and bell
peppers and mix well. Once the sausage is
cooked, add the egg mixture to the pan. Mix
well with the sausages.
5. Sprinkle with cheddar cheese and air fry
at 350 degrees F for another 5 minutes.
6. Serve hot with fresh tomato salsa for a
delicious low-carb breakfast.

Mozzarella Sticks

1 HOUR 20 MINUTES » MAKES 3 SERVINGS
AUTHENTIC ITALIAN CUISINE? NOT
EXACTLY. ABSOLUTELY DELICIOUS AND
A PARTY PLATTER MUST-HAVE? YOU BET
YOUR BUFALA.

1 lb mozzarella cheese
1 cup breadcrumbs
¼ cup white flour
3 Tbsp nonfat milk
2 eggs

1. Cut cheese into 3- by ½-inch sticks.
2. Place breadcrumbs, flour and the combined
milk and eggs each in separate bowls.
3. Dip cheese sticks in the flour, then
the egg-milk mixture and finally the
breadcrumbs.
4. Lay breaded sticks on a flat cookie sheet.
5. Freeze for 1 to 2 hours or until solid.
6. Place small batches of breaded sticks (do
not overcrowd) into the fry basket.
7. Scroll to the French Fries setting.
8. Cook for 12 minutes at 400 degrees F.

SHUTTERSTOCK

BBQ London Broil

2 HOURS 40 MINUTES » MAKES 6 SERVINGS

GET YOUR TASTE BUDS READY FOR A CLASSIC SUNDAY DINNER WITH THIS CAN'T FAIL BEEF DISH KICKED UP WITH HOMEMADE BBQ SAUCE.

2½ lbs London broil
¼ cup of your favorite BBQ sauce—OR use the following ingredients to make your own:
    2 Tbsp ketchup
    2 Tbsp steak sauce
    ¼ cup apple cider vinegar
    1-2 Tbsp Worcestershire sauce
    Salt & pepper, to taste
    1-2 Tbsp molasses (optional)

1. Add your BBQ sauce to a gallon size freezer bag.
2. Using your hands, squeeze the plastic bag to blend the ingredients.
3. Place the meat into the plastic bag and seal it. Be sure the marinade covers the meat. Set the bag on a plate and refrigerate at least 2 to 4 hours.
4. Give the fry basket a coating of non-stick cooking spray.
5. Remove the meat from the plastic bag, discard the marinade and place the meat on a plate. Using a paper towel, pat the meat gently to remove excess liquid. Place the steak in the basket and cook on the Steak setting.
6. Flip steak halfway through cooking time.

Classic Mac & Cheese

35 MINUTES » MAKES 4 SERVINGS

AFTER THEY TRY THIS VERSION OF THE HOMESTYLE FAVORITE, YOUR FAMILY WILL NEVER REACH FOR THE BLUE BOX AGAIN.

1 tsp cornstarch
2 cups shredded cheddar cheese, divided
2 cups heavy whipping cream
2 cups macaroni, dry

1. Mix the cornstarch with 1½ cups of the cheese.
2. Once they are combined, add the mixture to a large bowl with the cream and macaroni, reserving the rest of the cheese.
3. Pour into the baking pan and cover with foil. Place into the fry basket and then into the air fryer.
4. Scroll to the Bake setting.
5. Cook for 15 minutes at 310 degrees F.
6. Open and remove foil. Sprinkle the rest of the cheese on top.
7. Place the fry basket back into the air fryer.
8. Scroll to the Bake setting.
9. Cook for 10 minutes at 310 degrees F.

Grilled Cheese

10 MINUTES » MAKES 1 SERVING

WE BET YOU THOUGHT THERE WAS NO WAY TO MAKE THE HUMBLE GRILLED CHEESE EVEN BETTER THAN IT WAS BEFORE. BUT YOU NEVER THOUGHT TO AIR FRY IT.

2 slices of your favorite sandwich bread
2-3 slices yellow American or cheddar cheese
2 tsp butter

1. Place cheese between bread slices and butter the outside of each slice.
2. Place in air fryer and cook at 370 degrees F for 8 minutes, flipping halfway through.

Good Ol' Onion Rings

10 MINUTES » MAKES 6 SERVINGS

SURE, FRIES ARE GREAT AND ALL, BUT SOMETIMES THESE TANGY TREATS ARE CALLING YOUR NAME SO LOUD IT DROWNS OUT THE FRENCH FRY'S SONG.

1 bag frozen onion rings
  (Ore-Ida or your favorite)

1. Place onion rings in air fryer basket. Set temperature to 400 degrees F. Cook for 8 minutes for crispy onion rings. Note that you may have to fill your basket in multiple batches to ensure crispiness.
2. Flip contents of basket after 5 minutes, checking to be certain they aren't browning too much. Serve alongside (or as a topping on, we won't judge) your favorite burger or other sandwich.

Banana Bread

35 MINUTES » MAKES 1 LOAF

THE SATISFYING CONTRAST
BETWEEN CRISPY AND SOFT IS
ON FULL DISPLAY WHEN YOU MAKE
OUR UNIQUE BANANA BREAD.

¾ cup white-whole wheat flour
1 tsp cinnamon
½ tsp salt
¼ tsp baking soda
2 medium ripe mashed bananas
2 lightly beaten eggs
½ cup granulated sugar
⅓ cup plain nonfat yogurt
2 Tbsp vegetable oil
1 tsp vanilla extract
2 Tbsp chopped toasted walnuts

1. Cover the pan with parchment paper and
lightly coat with cooking spray.
2. Whisk together the flour, cinnamon, salt
and baking soda in a medium bowl; set aside.
3. In separate bowl, whisk together mashed
bananas, eggs, sugar, yogurt, oil and vanilla.
4. Gently stir wet ingredients into the flour
mixture until well combined.
5. Pour the mix into the pan and sprinkle
with walnuts.
6. Cook at 310 degrees F for 30 minutes.
7. Remove bread from the air fryer and let it
cool down for 15 minutes before slicing.

Chinese-Style Spare Ribs

40 MINUTES » MAKES 4-6 SERVINGS

COOK UP SOME OF YOUR FAVORITE EASTERN TREATS WITH YOUR AIR FRYER: YOU'LL NEVER HAVE TO LEAVE THE HOUSE!

1 Tbsp sesame oil
1 tsp minced garlic
1 tsp minced ginger
1 Tbsp fermented black bean paste
1 Tbsp Shaoxing Wine
1 Tbsp dark soy sauce
1 Tbsp agave nectar, or honey
1½ lbs spare ribs, cut into small pieces

1. In a large mixing bowl, stir together all wet ingredients.
2. Add the spare ribs and mix well. Allow the ribs to marinate for at least 30 minutes or up to 24 hours.
3. When you're ready to cook the ribs, remove from the marinade and place into the air fryer basket.
4. Set the air fryer at 375 degrees F for 8 minutes.
5. Check to ensure the ribs have an internal temperature of 165 degrees F before serving.

SHUTTERSTOCK

Chicken Nuggets

20 MINUTES » MAKES 4-6 SERVINGS

YOU'LL NEVER WANT TO GO BACK TO THE
DRIVE-THRU WINDOW AFTER YOU'VE
MADE YOUR OWN VERSION OF THESE FAST
FOOD CLASSICS.

1 cup buttermilk
2 lbs chicken tenders, cut into nugget size
2 eggs
1 cup flour
3 Tbsp grated Parmesan cheese
1 Tbsp paprika
1 Tbsp parsley flakes
Salt & pepper, to taste
2 cups panko breadcrumbs
Cooking spray

1. In a large bowl, mix the buttermilk with
the chicken.
2. Beat the eggs in a separate bowl.
3. In a third bowl, mix the flour, Parmesan
cheese, paprika, parsley, salt and pepper.
4. Dip each chicken nugget first in flour,
then in beaten egg and finally coat in
breadcrumbs.
5. Spray the basket with cooking spray.
6. Place the nuggets in the frying basket and
air fry at 400 degrees F for 10 minutes.
7. Halfway through you're cooking make sure
to carefully take out the basket and flip the
nuggets using a pair of tongs.

166 THE ULTIMATE AIR FRYER COOKBOOK

Old Fashioned Fish Sticks

30 MINUTES » MAKES 3 SERVINGS

THERE WAS ONLY ONE WAY TO MAKE THIS COMFORT FOOD EVEN MORE AMAZING: AIR FRY IT.

2 cups panko breadcrumbs
1 cup white flour
3 Tbsp milk
2 large eggs
1 lb cod
½ tsp black pepper
¼ tsp sea salt
Tartar sauce for dipping

1. Place breadcrumbs, flour and the combined milk and eggs each in separate bowls.
2. Cut fish into 3- by ½-inch sticks.
3. Season the fish with salt and pepper. Dip the fish sticks into the flour, then the egg mixture and finally the breadcrumbs.
4. Place fish sticks into the fry basket.
5. Scroll to the Fish setting.
6. Cook for 12 minutes at 350 degrees F, flipping the fish halfway through.
7. Serve with tartar sauce.

SHUTTERSTOCK

desserts

Leave room after your delicious air-fried main courses to show off the sweet tooth-sating potential of your new favorite appliance.

Churros
Recipe on page 176

Tasty Cupcakes

40 MINUTES » MAKES 2 SERVINGS
SURE, THERE'S ALWAYS THAT $10
CUPCAKE THE SIZE OF YOUR HEAD:
BUT THESE ARE BETTER FOR YOU,
AND COME WITH THE BENEFIT OF BEING
CLOSER TO ALL YOUR STUFF.

3½ oz caster sugar
¾ tsp baking powder
2 eggs
3 drops vanilla essence
3½ oz softened butter or margarine
3½ oz self-raising flour
Food coloring and other garnishes of your
    choice (optional)

1. Place all the ingredients into a bowl and
use a hand mixer to whisk ingredients
together until light and creamy.
2. Fill your silicone cupcake molds half full of
the mixture.
3. Place the cakes inside the fry basket. Set
the timer for 20 minutes and cook at 350
degrees F.
4. Keep an eye on them for over-browning
and check if they're cooked by pressing one
gently: if it rises back up it is cooked.
5. Once cooked, carefully remove the insert
and place it onto roasting rack to cool. After
five minutes remove the cakes from the inner
bowl and cool them for a further 15 minutes
on a roasting rack before decorating.

Chocolate Cake

40 MINUTES » MAKES 2 SERVINGS

EVEN YOUR PICKIEST GUESTS WILL AGREE THIS DESSERT IS A HIT NO MATTER WHEN IT'S SERVED.

3 eggs
½ cup sour cream
1 cup flour
²/₃ cup sugar
1 stick butter, room temperature
¹/₃ cup cocoa powder
1 tsp baking powder
½ tsp baking soda
2 tsp vanilla

1. Preheat air fryer to 320 degrees F.
2. Mix ingredients in a stand mixer on low.
3. Pour into cake carrel.
4. Place in the air fryer basket and cook for 25 minutes.
5. Once timer rings, use a toothpick to see if cake is done.
6. Cool cake on a wire rack.
7. Ice with your favorite frosting.

Peach Hand Pies

30 MINUTES » MAKES 3 SERVINGS

YOU DON'T NEED A FRONT PORCH, ROCKING CHAIR OR TALL GLASS OF SWEET TEA TO ENJOY THESE PIES, BUT IT CERTAINLY DOES PUT YOU IN A FINE MOOD.

2 (5-oz) fresh peaches, peeled and chopped
1 Tbsp fresh lemon juice (from 1 lemon)
3 Tbsp granulated sugar
1 tsp vanilla extract
¼ tsp table salt
1 tsp cornstarch
1 (14.1-oz) pkg. refrigerated pie crusts
Cooking spray

1. Stir together peaches, lemon juice, sugar, vanilla and salt in a medium bowl. Let stand 15 minutes, stirring occasionally. Drain peaches, reserving 1 Tbsp liquid. Whisk cornstarch into reserved liquid; stir into drained peaches.
2. Cut pie crusts into 8 (4-inch) circles. Place about 1 Tbsp filling in center of each circle. Brush edges of dough with water; fold dough over filling to form half-moons. Crimp edges with a fork to seal; cut 3 small slits in top of pies. Coat pies well with cooking spray.
3. Place 3 pies in a single layer in the air fryer basket, and cook at 350 degrees F until golden brown, 12 to 14 minutes. Repeat with remaining pies.

off

THE ULTIMATE AIR FRYER COOKBOOK **175**

Churros

35 MINUTES » MAKES 3 SERVINGS
YOU LOVE THE DEEP FRIED VERSION ON SPECIAL OCCASIONS, AND NOW YOU CAN ENJOY THE AIR-FRIED VERSION AT HOME— HOLD THE GUILT.

6 Tbsp unsalted butter
2¼ cups water
1 tsp salt
1 tsp vanilla extract
2¼ cups all-purpose flour
1 large egg
1 cup sugar
2 tsp ground cinnamon

1. In a medium saucepan over medium-high heat, melt butter then add water, salt and vanilla. Bring to a boil and remove from the heat.
2. Add the flour and stir the mixture with a wooden spoon until a smooth dough is formed. (It should be almost like the texture of homemade play dough.)
3. Let the dough cool for about 15 minutes then transfer to a bowl and add the egg. Stir quickly until egg is mixed in.
4. Transfer dough to a piping bag fitted with a 1M tip.
5. Pipe several 6-inch sticks of churro dough into the air fryer making sure they don't touch.
6. Bake at 380 degrees F for 10 minutes.
7. While the churros are cooking you can make the cinnamon sugar mixture by combining the two in a bowl and mixing. Sprinkle over cooked churros and serve.

Desserts

Pumpkin Spice Bread

35 MINUTES » MAKES 4-6 SERVINGS

THERE'S A GOOD REASON PUMPKIN SPICE SEEMS TO BE IN EVERYTHING THESE DAYS: IT'S DELICIOUS!

¼ lb butter (melted)
3½ oz brown sugar
¼ lb pumpkin puree
1 oz Greek yogurt
Cinnamon, to taste
Cardamon, to taste
Allspice, to taste
Salt, to taste
A splash of whiskey
2 eggs
6 oz flour
½ oz baking soda

For Plating:
Caramel ice cream
Grated macadamia nuts
Pumpkin puree

1. In a bowl mix the melted butter, brown sugar, pumpkin puree and Greek yogurt. Add cinnamon, cardamom, allspice and salt to taste. Add whiskey and eggs, already whisked in a separate bowl, and mix.
2. Combine the flour with the baking soda. Combine with previous mixture and mix well.
3. Using a mini cake silicone pan, dump the mixture, filling up each hole in the pan. It's going to be messy, so make sure to clean the borders first before inserting the silicone pan in the air fryer. Bake for 25 minutes at 350 degrees F. Use a knife to check if the bread is fully cooked (the knife should come out clean). If not, keep cooking for an extra 3 to 5 minutes.
4. Plate your Pumpkin Spice Bread with a serving of caramel ice cream and a side of pumpkin puree and sprinkle with grated macadamia nuts before serving.

SHUTTERSTOCK

Apple Pie

30 MINUTES » MAKES 2 SERVINGS
AS AMERICAN AS BASEBALL AND JAZZ,
THIS DESSERT WILL KEEP THEM COMING
BACK FOR MORE, À LA MODE OR NOT.

1 red apple
1 green apple
1 Tbsp cinnamon
3 Tbsp white sugar
3 Tbsp brown sugar
1 Tbsp apple cider vinegar
1 cup flour
½ Tbsp sugar
½ tsp salt
3 Tbsp butter
3 Tbsp lard or shortening
3-4 Tbsp ice water

1. Chop your apples into tiny pieces and
combine all filling ingredients through to the
vinegar together in a large bowl. Set aside to
let the flavor develop.
2. To make your pie crust, mix the flour,
sugar, salt, butter and shortening together
with a fork or your hands.
3. Add 3 Tbsp of water and knead, adding
more to get a cohesive dough.
4. Roll out your pie crust to a ½-inch
thickness and then cut into your desired
pie shapes.
5. Spoon 1 Tbsp of the filling into the center
of half of the pie shapes, and then place
a second pie crust shape overtop. Press
around the edges to seal.
6. Place in the air fryer and add oil to the
dispenser.
7. Bake at 360 degrees F for 7 to 10 minutes,
watching carefully.

Vegan Small-Batch Brownies

35 MINUTES » MAKES 2 SERVINGS

AFTER ONE TASTE OF THESE AIR-FRYER PHENOMS, EVERYONE WILL BE CALLING THESE YOUR "SPECIAL BROWNIES."

WET INGREDIENTS
¼ cup non dairy milk
¼ cup aquafaba
½ tsp vanilla extract

DRY INGREDIENTS
½ cup whole wheat pastry flour
½ cup vegan sugar
   (or sweetener of choice, to taste)
¼ cup cocoa powder
1 Tbsp ground flax seeds
¼ tsp salt

MIX-INS
¼ cup of any one or a combination of the following: chopped walnuts, hazelnuts, pecans, mini vegan chocolate chips, shredded coconut

1. Mix the dry ingredients together in one bowl. Then mix the wet ingredients in a large measuring cup. Add the wet to the dry and mix well.
2. Add in the mix-in(s) of your choice and mix again.
3. Preheat your air fryer to 350 degrees F. Either spray some oil on a 5-inch cake or pie round pan (or a loaf pan that fits in your air fryer), or line it with parchment paper to keep it completely oil-free.
4. Place the pan in the fryer basket. Cook for 20 minutes on the Bake setting. If the middle is not well set or a knife doesn't come out clean when stuck in the middle cook for 5 minutes more and repeat as needed.

Desserts

Cinnamon Donut Bites

40 MINUTES » MAKES 3 SERVINGS
EVER WANT A WHOLE DONUT BUT ALSO
WANT TO SAVE SOME ROOM FOR OTHER
PARTY SNACKS? YOU'RE IN LUCK. BEHOLD:
HOMEMADE DONUT HOLES.

²/₃ cup all-purpose flour
²/₃ cup whole-wheat flour
2 Tbsp granulated sugar
1 tsp baking powder
¼ tsp ground cinnamon
¼ tsp kosher salt
4 Tbsp cold salted butter, cut into small pieces
¹/₃ cup whole milk
Cooking spray
2 cups (about 8 oz.) powdered sugar
3 Tbsp water

1. Whisk together flours, granulated sugar,
baking powder, cinnamon and salt.
2. Add butter; cut into mixture using 2
knives or a pastry cutter until butter is well
combined with flour and mixture resembles
coarse cornmeal. Add milk and stir together
until dough forms a ball. Place dough on a
floured surface and knead until dough is
smooth and forms a cohesive ball, about
30 seconds. Cut dough into 16 equal pieces.
Gently roll each piece into a smooth ball.
3. Coat air fryer basket well with cooking
spray. Place 8 balls in the fryer basket,
leaving room between each.
4. Spray donut balls with cooking spray.
Cook at 350 degrees F until browned and
puffed, 10 to 12 minutes. Gently remove
donut balls from basket, and place on a wire
rack over foil. Let cool 5 minutes. Repeat
with remaining donut balls.
5. Whisk powdered sugar and water in a
medium bowl until smooth. Spoon half of the
glaze over donut balls. Let cool and sprinkle
with cinnamon sugar if desired.

Index

Index

Conversion Chart

VOLUME

¼ teaspoon	=	1.25 mL
½ teaspoon	=	2.75 mL
1 teaspoon	=	5 mL
1 tablespoon	=	15 mL
¼ cup	=	60 mL
⅓ cup	=	80 mL
½ cup	=	120 mL
⅔ cup	=	160 mL
¾ cup	=	180 mL
1 cup	=	240 mL
1 quart	=	1 liter
1½ quarts	=	1.5 liters
2 quarts	=	2 liters
2½ quarts	=	2.5 liters
3 quarts	=	3 liters
4 quarts	=	4 liters

WEIGHT

1 ounce	=	30 grams
2 ounces	=	55 grams
3 ounces	=	85 grams
4 ounces (¼ pound)	=	115 grams
8 ounces (½ pound)	=	225 grams
16 ounces (1 pound)	=	455 grams
2 pounds	=	910 grams

LENGTH

⅛ inch	=	3 mm
¼ inch	=	6 mm
½ inch	=	13 mm
¾ inch	=	19 mm
1 inch	=	2.5 cm
2 inches	=	5 cm

TEMPERATURES

Fahrenheit		Celsius
32°	=	0°
212°	=	100°
250°	=	120°
275°	=	140°
300°	=	150°
325°	=	160°
350°	=	180°
375°	=	190°
400°	=	200°
425°	=	220°
450°	=	230°
475°	=	250°
500°	=	260°

Topix Media Lab
For inquiries, call 646-838-6637

Copyright 2021 Topix Media Lab

Published by Topix Media Lab
14 Wall Street, Suite 4B
New York, NY 10005

Printed in China

Note to our readers
The information in this book has been carefully researched, and every reasonable effort has been made to ensure its accuracy. Neither the book's publisher nor its creators assume any responsibility for any accidents, injuries, losses or other damages that might come from its use. You are solely responsible for taking any and all reasonable and necessary precautions when performing the activities detailed in its pages.

ISBN 13: 978-1-948174-76-3
ISBN 10: 1-948174-76-6

CEO Tony Romando

Vice President & Publisher Phil Sexton
Senior Vice President of Sales & New Markets Tom Mifsud
Vice President of Retail Sales & Logistics Linda Greenblatt
Director of Finance Vandana Patel
Manufacturing Director Nancy Puskuldjian
Financial Analyst Matthew Quinn
Brand Marketing & Promotions Assistant Emily McBride

Chief Content Officer Jeff Ashworth
Director of Editorial Operations Courtney Kerrigan
Creative Director Steven Charny
Photo Director Dave Weiss

Content Editor Tim Baker
Content Designer Kelsey Payne
Art Director Susan Dazzo
Senior Editor Trevor Courneen
Associate Editor Juliana Sharaf
Copy Editor & Fact Checker Tara Sherman

Co-Founders Bob Lee, Tony Romando

Recipes supplied by Yedi Houseware Appliances

Indexing by R studio T, NYC

TM21-01